Dramatic Lyrics

Robert Browning

CONTENTS

Dramatic Lyrics

CAVALIER TUNES

MARCHING ALONG

Kentish Sir Byng stood for his King,
Bidding the crop-headed Parliament swing:
And, pressing a troop unable to stoop
And see the rogues flourish and honest folk droop,
Marched them along, fifty-score strong,
Great-hearted gentlemen, singing this song.

God for King Charles! Pym and such carles
To the Devil that prompts `em their treasonous parles!
Cavaliers, up! Lips from the cup,
Hands from the pasty, nor bite take nor sup
Till you`re—-

CHORUS.—-Marching along, fifty-score strong,
     Great-hearted gentlemen, singing this song.

Hampden to hell, and his obsequies` knell
Serve Hazelrig, Fiennes, and young Harry as well!
England, good cheer! Rupert is near!
Kentish and loyalists, keep we not here

CHORUS.—-Marching along, fifty-score strong,
     Great-hearted gentlemen, singing this song?

Then, God for King Charles! Pym and his snarls
To the Devil that pricks on such pestilent carles!
Hold by the right, you double your might;
So, onward to Nottingham, fresh for the fight,

CHORUS.—-March we along, fifty-score strong,
     Great-hearted gentlemen, singing this song!

GIVE A ROUSE

King Charles, and who'll do him right now?
King Charles, and who's ripe for fight now?
Give a rouse: here's, in hell's despite now,
King Charles!

Who gave me the goods that went since?
Who raised me the house that sank once?
Who helped me to gold I spent since?
Who found me in wine you drank once?

CHORUS.—-King Charles, and who'll do him right now?
King Charles, and who's ripe for fight now?
Give a rouse: here's, in hell's despite now,
King Charles!

To whom used my boy George quaff else,
By the old fool's side that begot him?
For whom did he cheer and laugh else,
While Noll's damned troopers shot him?

CHORUS.—-King Charles, and who'll do him right now?
King Charles, and who's ripe for fight now?
Give a rouse: here's, in hell's despite now,
King Charles!

BOOT AND SADDLE

Boot, saddle, to horse, and away!
Rescue my castle before the hot day
Brightens to blue from its silvery grey,

CHORUS.—-Boot, saddle, to horse, and away!

Ride past the suburbs, asleep as you`d say;
Many`s the friend there, will listen and pray
``God`s luck to gallants that strike up the lay—-

CHORUS.—-``Boot, saddle, to horse, and away!``

Forty miles off, like a roebuck at bay,
Flouts Castle Brancepeth the Roundheads` array:
Who laughs, ``Good fellows ere this, by my fay,

CHORUS.—-``Boot, saddle, to horse, and away!``

Who? My wife Gertrude; that, honest and gay,
Laughs when you talk of surrendering, ``Nay!
``I`ve better counsellors; what counsel they?

CHORUS.—-"Boot, saddle, to horse, and away!"

THE LOST LEADER

Just for a handful of silver he left us,
  Just for a riband to stick in his coat—-
Found the one gift of which fortune bereft us,
  Lost all the others she lets us devote;
They, with the gold to give, doled him out silver,
  So much was theirs who so little allowed:
How all our copper had gone for his service!
  Rags—-were they purple, his heart had been proud!
We that had loved him so, followed him, honoured him,
  Lived in his mild and magnificent eye,
Learned his great language, caught his clear accents,
  Made him our pattern to live and to die!
Shakespeare was of us, Milton was for us,
  Burns, Shelley, were with us,—-they watch from their graves!
He alone breaks from the van and the free-men,
  —-He alone sinks to the rear and the slaves!

We shall march prospering,—-not thro` his presence;
  Songs may inspirit us,—-not from his lyre;
Deeds will be done,—-while he boasts his quiescence,
  Still bidding crouch whom the rest bade aspire:
Blot out his name, then, record one lost soul more,
  One task more declined, one more foot-path untrod,
One more devils`-triumph and sorrow for angels,
  One wrong more to man, one more insult to God!
Life`s night begins: let him never come back to us!
  There would be doubt, hesitation and pain,
Forced praise on our part—-the glimmer of twilight,
  Never glad confident morning again!
Best fight on well, for we taught him—-strike gallantly,
  Menace our heart ere we master his own;
Then let him receive the new knowledge and wait us,
  Pardoned in heaven, the first by the throne!

"HOW THEY BROUGHT THE GOOD NEWS FROM GHENT TO AIX."

I sprang to the stirrup, and Joris, and he;
I galloped, Dirck galloped, we galloped all three;
``Good speed!`` cried the watch, as the gate-bolts undrew;
``Speed!`` echoed the wall to us galloping through;
Behind shut the postern, the lights sank to rest,
And into the midnight we galloped abreast.

Not a word to each other; we kept the great pace
Neck by neck, stride by stride, never changing our place;
I turned in my saddle and made its girths tight,
Then shortened each stirrup, and set the pique right,
Rebuckled the cheek-strap, chained slacker the bit,
Nor galloped less steadily Roland a whit.

`Twas moonset at starting; but while we drew near
Lokeren, the cocks crew and twilight dawned clear;
At Boom, a great yellow star came out to see;
At Dffeld,`twas morning as plain as could be;
And from Mecheln church-steeple we heard the half-chime,
So, Joris broke silence with, ``Yet there is time!``

At Aershot, up leaped of a sudden the sun,
And against him the cattle stood black every one,
To stare thro` the mist at us galloping past,
And I saw my stout galloper Roland at last,
With resolute shoulders, each hutting away
The haze, as some bluff river headland its spray:

And his low head and crest, just one sharp ear bent back
For my voice, and the other pricked out on his track;
And one eye`s black intelligence, —-ever that glance
O`er its white edge at me, his own master, askance!

And the thick heavy spume-flakes which aye and anon
His fierce lips shook upwards in galloping on.

By Hasselt, Dirck groaned; and cried Joris, ``Stay spur!
``Your Roos galloped bravely, the fault`s not in her,
``We`ll remember at Aix``—-for one heard the quick wheeze
Of her chest, saw the stretched neck and staggering knees,
And sunk tail, and horrible heave of the flank,
As down on her haunches she shuddered and sank.

So, we were left galloping, Joris and I,
Past Looz and past Tongres, no cloud in the sky;
The broad sun above laughed a pitiless laugh,
`Neath our feet broke the brittle bright stubble like chaff;
Till over by Dalhem a dome-spire sprang white,
And ``Gallop,`` gasped Joris, ``for Aix is in sight!``

``How they`ll greet us!``—-and all in a moment his roan
Rolled neck and croup over, lay dead as a stone;
And there was my Roland to bear the whole weight
Of the news which alone could save Aix from her fate,
With his nostrils like pits full of blood to the brim,
And with circles of red for his eye-sockets` rim.

Then I cast loose my buffcoat, each holster let fall,
Shook off both my jack-boots, let go belt and all,
Stood up in the stirrup, leaned, patted his ear,
Called my Roland his pet-name, my horse without peer;
Clapped my hands, laughed and sang, any noise, bad or good,
Till at length into Aix Roland galloped and stood.

And all I remember is—-friends flocking round
As I sat with his head `twixt my knees on the ground;
And no voice but was praising this Roland of mine,
As I poured down his throat our last measure of wine,
Which (the burgesses voted by common consent)
Was no more than his due who brought good news from Ghent.

THROUGH THE METIDJA TO ABD-EL-KADR

As I ride, as I ride,
With a full heart for my guide,
So its tide rocks my side,
As I ride, as I ride,
That, as I were double-eyed,
He, in whom our Tribes confide,
Is descried, ways untried
As I ride, as I ride.

As I ride, as I ride
To our Chief and his Allied,
Who dares chide my heart`s pride
As I ride, as I ride?
Or are witnesses denied—-
Through the desert waste and wide
Do I glide unespied
As I ride, as I ride?

As I ride, as I ride,
When an inner voice has cried,
The sands slide, nor abide
(As I ride, as I ride)
O`er each visioned homicide
That came vaunting (has he lied?)
To reside—-where he died,
As I ride, as I ride.

As I ride, as I ride,
Ne`er has spur my swift horse plied,
Yet his hide, streaked and pied,
As I ride, as I ride,
Shows where sweat has sprung and dried,
—-Zebra-footed, ostrich-thighed—-

How has vied stride with stride
As I ride, as I ride!

As I ride, as I ride,
Could I loose what Fate has tied,
Ere I pried, she should hide
(As I ride, as I ride)
All that's meant me—-satisfied
When the Prophet and the Bride
Stop veins I'd have subside
As I ride, as I ride!

NATIONALITY IN DRINKS

My heart sank with our Claret-flask,
  Just now, beneath the heavy sedges
That serve this Pond`s black face for mask
  And still at yonder broken edges
O` the hole, where up the bubbles glisten,
After my heart I look and listen.

Our laughing little flask, compelled
  Thro` depth to depth more bleak and shady;
As when, both arms beside her held,
  Feet straightened out, some gay French lady
Is caught up from life`s light and motion,
And dropped into death`s silent ocean!

Up jumped Tokay on our table,
Like a pygmy castle-warder,
Dwarfish to see, but stout and able,
Arms and accoutrements all in order;
And fierce he looked North, then, wheeling South,
Blew with his bugle a challenge to Drouth,
Cocked his flap-hat with the tosspot-feather,
Twisted his thumb in his red moustache,
Jingled his huge brass spurs together,
Tightened his waist with its Buda sash,
And then, with an impudence nought could abash,
Shrugged his hump-shoulder, to tell the beholder,
For twenty such knaves he should laugh but the bolder:
And so, with his sword-hilt gallantly jutting,
And dexter-hand on his haunch abutting,
Went the little man, Sir Ausbruch, strutting!

Here`s to Nelson`s memory!
`Tis the second time that I, at sea,
Right off Cape Trafalgar here,

Have drunk it deep in British Beer.
Nelson for ever—-any time
Am I his to command in prose or rhyme!
Give me of Nelson only a touch,
And I save it, be it little or much:
Here`s one our Captain gives, and so
Down at the word, by George, shall it go!
He says that at Greenwich they point the beholder
To Nelson`s coat, ``still with tar on the shoulder:
``For he used to lean with one shoulder digging,
``Jigging, as it were, and zig-zag-zigging
``Up against the mizen-rigging!``

GARDEN FANCIES

THE FLOWER`S NAME

Here`s the garden she walked across,
  Arm in my arm, such a short while since:
Hark, now I push its wicket, the moss
  Hinders the hinges and makes them wince!
She must have reached this shrub ere she turned,
  As back with that murmur the wicket swung;
For she laid the poor snail, my chance foot spurned,
  To feed and forget it the leaves among.

Down this side ofthe gravel-walk
  She went while her rope`s edge brushed the box:
And here she paused in her gracious talk
  To point me a moth on the milk-white phlox.
Roses, ranged in valiant row,
  I will never think that she passed you by!
She loves you noble roses, I know;
  But yonder, see, where the rock-plants lie!

This flower she stopped at, finger on lip,
  Stooped over, in doubt, as settling its claim;
Till she gave me, with pride to make no slip,
  Its soft meandering Spanish name:
What a name! Was it love or praise?
  Speech half-asleep or song half-awake?
I must learn Spanish, one of these days,
  Only for that slow sweet name`s sake.

Roses, if I live and do well,
  I may bring her, one of these days,
To fix you fast with as fine a spell,
  Fit you each with his Spanish phrase;
But do not detain me now; for she lingers

There, like sunshine over the ground,
And ever I see her soft white fingers
　　Searching after the bud she found.

Flower, you Spaniard, look that you grow not,
　　Stay as you are and be loved for ever!
Bud, if I kiss you `tis that you blow not:
　　Mind, the shut pink mouth opens never!
For while it pouts, her fingers wrestle,
　　Twinkling the audacious leaves between,
Till round they turn and down they nestle—-
　　Is not the dear mark still to be seen?

Where I find her not, beauties vanish;
　　Whither I follow ber, beauties flee;
Is there no method to tell her in Spanish
　　June`s twice June since she breathed it with me?
Come, bud, show me the least of her traces,
　　Treasure my lady`s lightest footfall!
—-Ah, you may flout and turn up your faces—-
　　Roses, you are not so fair after all!

SIBRANDUS SCHAFNABURGENSIS

Plague take all your pedants, say I!
　　He who wrote what I hold in my hand,
Centuries back was so good as to die,
　　Leaving this rubbish to cumber the land;
This, that was a book in its time,
　　Printed on paper and bound in leather,
Last month in the white of a matin-prime
　　Just when the birds sang all together.

Into the garden I brought it to read,
　　And under the arbute and laurustine
Read it, so help me grace in my need,

From title-page to closing line.
Chapter on chapter did I count,
  As a curious traveller counts Stonehenge;
Added up the mortal amount;
  And then proceeded to my revenge.

Yonder`s a plum-tree with a crevice
  An owl would build in, were he but sage;
For a lap of moss, like a fine pont-levis
  In a castle of the Middle Age,
Joins to a lip of gum, pure amber;
  When he`d be private, there might he spend
Hours alone in his lady`s chamber:
  Into this crevice I dropped our friend.

Splash, went he, as under he ducked,
  —-At the bottom, I knew, rain-drippings stagnate:
Next, a handful of blossoms I plucked
  To bury him with, my bookshelf`s magnate;
Then I went in-doors, brought out a loaf,
  Half a cheese, and a bottle of Chablis;
Lay on the grass and forgot the oaf
  Over a jolly chapter of Rabelais.

Now, this morning, betwixt the moss
  And gum that locked our friend in limbo,
A spider had spun his web across,
  And sat in the midst with arms akimbo:
So, I took pity, for learning`s sake,
  And, *de profundis, accentibus ltis,*
Cantate! quoth I, as I got a rake;
  And up I fished his delectable treatise.

Here you have it, dry in the sun,
  With all the binding all of a blister,
And great blue spots where the ink has run,
  And reddish streaks that wink and glister
O`er the page so beautifully yellow:

Oh, well have the droppings played their tricks!
Did he guess how toadstools grow, this fellow?
  Here's one stuck in his chapter six!

How did he like it when the live creatures
  Tickled and toused and browsed him all over,
And worm, slug, eft, with serious features,
  Came in, each one, for his right of trover?
—-When the water-beetle with great blind deaf face
  Made of her eggs the stately deposit,
And the newt borrowed just so much of the preface
  As tiled in the top of his black wife's closet?

All that life and fun and romping,
  All that frisking and twisting and coupling,
While slowly our poor friend's leaves were swamping
  And clasps were cracking and covers suppling!
As if you bad carried sour John Knox
  To the play-house at Paris, Vienna or Munich,
Fastened him into a front-row box,
  And danced off the ballet with trousers and tunic.

Come, old martyr! What, torment enough is it?
  Back to my room shall you take your sweet self.
Good-bye, mother-beetle; husband-eft, *sufficit!*
  See the snug niche I have made on my shelf!
A.'s book shall prop you up, B.'s shall cover you,
  Here's C. to be grave with, or D. to be gay,
And with E. on each side, and F. right over you,
  Dry-rot at ease till the Judgment-day!

SOLILOQUY OF THE SPANISH CLOISTER

Gr-r-r—-there go, my heart's abhorrence!
  Water your damned flower-pots, do!
If hate killed men, Brother Lawrence,
  God's blood, would not mine kill you!
What? your myrtle-bush wants trimming?
  Oh, that rose has prior claims—-
Needs its leaden vase filled brimming?
  Hell dry you up with its flames!

At the meal we sit together:
  Salve tibi! I must hear
Wise talk of the kind of weather,
  Sort of season, time of year:
Not a plenteous cork-crop: scarcely
  Dare we hope oak-galls, I doubt:
What's the Latin name for ``parsley``?
  What's the Greek name for Swine's Snout?

Whew! We'll have our platter burnished,
  Laid with care on our own shelf!
With a fire-new spoon we're furnished,
  And a goblet for ourself,
Rinsed like something sacrificial
  Ere 'tis fit to touch our chaps—-
Marked with L. for our initial!
  (He-he! There his lily snaps!)

Saint, forsooth! While brown Dolores
  Squats outside the Convent bank
With Sanchicha, telling stories,
  Steeping tresses in the tank,
Blue-black, lustrous, thick like horsehairs,
  —-Can't I see his dead eye glow,

Bright as 'twere a Barbary corsair's?
  (That is, if he'd let it show!)

When he finishes refection,
  Knife and fork he never lays
Cross-wise, to my recollection,
  As do I, in Jesu's praise.
I the Trinity illustrate,
  Drinking watered orange-pulp—-
In three sips the Arian frustrate;
  While he drains his at one gulp.

Oh, those melons? If he's able
  We're to have a feast! so nice!
One goes to the Abbot's table,
  All of us get each a slice.
How go on your flowers? None double
  Not one fruit-sort can you spy?
Strange!—-And I, too, at such trouble,
  Keep them close-nipped on the sly!

There's a great text in Galatians,
  Once you trip on it, entails
Twenty-nine distinct damnations,
  One sure, if another fails:
If I trip him just a-dying,
  Sure of heaven as sure can be,
Spin him round and send him flying
  Off to hell, a Manichee?

Or, my scrofulous French novel
  On grey paper with blunt type!
Simply glance at it, you grovel
  Hand and foot in Belial's gripe:
If I double down its pages
  At the woeful sixteenth print,
When he gathers his greengages,
  Ope a sieve and slip it in't?

Or, there`s Satan!—-one might venture
  Pledge one`s soul to him, yet leave
Such a flaw in the indenture
  As he`d miss till, past retrieve,
Blasted lay that rose-acacia
  We`re so proud of! *Hy, Zy, Hine* ...
`St, there`s Vespers! *Plena gratitude*
  Ave, Virgo! Gr-r-r—-you swine!

THE LABORATORY

Now that I, tying thy glass mask tightly,
May gaze thro` these faint smokes curling whitely,
As thou pliest thy trade in this devil`s-smithy—-
Which is the poison to poison her, prithee?

He is with her, and they know that I know
Where they are, what they do: they believe my tears flow
While they laugh, laugh at me, at me fled to the drear
Empty church, to pray God in, for them!—-I am here.

Grind away, moisten and mash up thy paste,
Pound at thy powder,—-I am not in haste!
Better sit thus, and observe thy strange things,
Than go where men wait me and dance at the King`s.

That in the mortar—-you call it a gum?
Ah, the brave tree whence such gold oozings come!
And yonder soft phial, the exquisite blue,
Sure to taste sweetly,—-is that poison too?

Had I but all of them, thee and thy treasures,
What a wild crowd of invisible pleasures!
To carry pure death in an earring, a casket,
A signet, a fan-mount, a filigree basket!

Soon, at the King`s, a mere lozenge to give,
And Pauline should have just thirty minutes to live!
But to light a pastile, and Elise, with her head
And her breast and her arms and her hands, should drop dead!

Quick—-is it finished? The colour`s too grim!
Why not soft like the phial`s, enticing and dim?
Let it brighten her drink, let her turn it and stir,
And try it and taste, ere she fix and prefer!

Dramatic Lyrics

What a drop! She`s not little, no minion like me!
That`s why she ensnared him: this never will free
The soul from those masculine eyes, —-Say, ``no!``
To that pulse`s magnificent come-and-go.

For only last night, as they whispered, I brought
My own eyes to bear on her so, that I thought
Could I keep them one half minute fixed, she would fall
Shrivelled; she fell not; yet this does it all!

Not that I bid you spare her the pain;
Let death be felt and the proof remain:
Brand, burn up, bite into its grace—-
He is sure to remember her dying face!

Is it done? Take my mask off! Nay, be not morose;
It kills her, and this prevents seeing it close;
The delicate droplet, my whole fortune`s fee!
If it hurts her, beside, can it ever hurt me?

Now, take all my jewels, gorge gold to your fill,
You may kiss me, old man, on my mouth if you will!
But brush this dust off me, lest horror it brings
Ere I know it—-next moment I dance at the King`s!

THE CONFESSIONAL

It is a lie—-their Priests, their Pope,
Their Saints, their ... all they fear or hope
Are lies, and lies—-there! through my door
And ceiling, there! and walls and floor,
There, lies, they lie—-shall still be hurled
Till spite of them I reach the world!

You think Priests just and holy men!
Before they put me in this den
I was a human creature too,
With flesh and blood like one of you,
A girl that laughed in beauty`s pride
Like lilies in your world outside.

I had a lover—-shame avaunt!
This poor wrenched body, grim and gaunt,
Was kissed all over till it burned,
By lips the truest, love e`er turned
His heart`s own tint: one night they kissed
My soul out in a burning mist.

So, next day when the accustomed train
Of things grew round my sense again,
``That is a sin,`` I said: and slow
With downcast eyes to church I go,
And pass to the confession-chair,
And tell the old mild father there.

But when I falter Beltran`s name,
``Ha?`` quoth the father; ``much I blame
``The sin; yet wherefore idly grieve?
``Despair not—-strenuously retrieve!
``Nay, I will turn this love of thine
``To lawful love, almost divine;

``For he is young, and led astray,
``This Beltran, and he schemes, men say,
``To change the laws of church and state
``So, thine shall be an angel`s fate,
``Who, ere the thunder breaks, should roll
``Its cloud away and save his soul.

``For, when he lies upon thy breast,
``Thou mayst demand and be possessed
``Of all his plans, and next day steal
``To me, and all those plans reveal,
``That I and every priest, to purge
``His soul, may fast and use the scourge.``

That father`s beard was long and white,
With love and truth his brow seemed bright;
I went back, all on fire with joy,
And, that same evening, bade the boy
Tell me, as lovers should, heart-free,
Something to prove his love of me.

He told me what he would not tell
For hope of heaven or fear of hell;
And I lay listening in such pride!
And, soon as he had left my side,
Tripped to the church by morning-light
To save his soul in his despite.

I told the father all his schemes,
Who were his comrades, what their dreams;
``And now make haste,`` I said, ``to pray
``The one spot from his soul away;
``To-night he comes, but not the same
``Will look!`` At night he never came.

Nor next night: on the after-morn,
I went forth with a strength new-born.
The church was empty; something drew

21

My steps into the street; I knew
It led me to the market-place:
Where, lo, on high, the father`s face!

That horrible black scaffold dressed,
That stapled block ... God sink the rest!
That head strapped back, that blinding vest,
Those knotted hands and naked breast,
Till near one busy hangman pressed,
And, on the neck these arms caressed ...

No part in aught they hope or fear!
No heaven with them, no hell!—-and here,
No earth, not so much space as pens
My body in their worst of dens
But shall bear God and man my cry,
Lies—-lies, again—-and still, they lie!

CRISTINA

She should never have looked at me
  If she meant I should not love her!
There are plenty ... men, you call such,
  I suppose ... she may discover
All her soul to, if she pleases,
  And yet leave much as she found them:
But I`m not so, and she knew it
  When she fixed me, glancing round them,

What? To fix me thus meant nothing?
  But I can`t tell (there`s my weakness)
What her look said!—-no vile cant, sure,
  About ``need to strew the bleakness
``Of some lone shore with its pearl-seed.
  ``That the sea feels``—-no strange yearning
``That such souls have, most to lavish
  ``Where there`s chance of least returning.``

Oh, we`re sunk enough here, God knows!
  But not quite so sunk that moments,
Sure tho` seldom, are denied us,
  When the spirit`s true endowments
Stand out plainly from its false ones,
  And apprise it if pursuing
Or the right way or the wrong way,
  To its triumph or undoing.

There are flashes struck from midnights,
  There are fire-flames noondays kindle,
Whereby piled-up honours perish,
  Whereby swollen ambitions dwindle,
While just this or that poor impulse,
  Which for once had play unstifled,

Seems the sole work of a life-time
  That away the rest have trifled.

Doubt you if, in some such moment,
  As she fixed me, she felt clearly,
Ages past the soul existed,
  Here an age 'tis resting merely,
And hence fleets again for ages,
  While the true end, sole and single,
It stops here for is, this love-way,
  With some other soul to mingle?

Else it loses what it lived for,
  And eternally must lose it;
Better ends may be in prospect,
  Deeper blisses (if you choose it),
But this life's end and this love-bliss
  Have been lost here. Doubt you whether
This she felt as, looking at me,
  Mine and her souls rushed together?

Oh, observe! Of course, next moment,
  The world's honours, in derision,
Trampled out the light for ever:
  Never fear but there's provision
Of the devil's to quench knowledge
  Lest we walk the earth in rapture!
—-Making those who catch God's secret
  Just so much more prize their capture!

Such am I: the secret's mine now!
  She has lost me, I have gained her;
Her soul's mine: and thus, grown perfect,
  I shall pass my life's remainder.
Life will just hold out the proving
  Both our powers, alone and blended:
And then, come next life quickly!
  This world's use will have been ended.

THE LOST MISTRESS

All`s over, then: does truth sound bitter
　As one at first believes?
Hark, `tis the sparrows` good-night twitter
　About your cottage eaves!

And the leaf-buds on the vine are woolly,
　I noticed that, to-day;
One day more bursts them open fully
　—-You know the red turns grey.

To-morrow we meet the same then, dearest?
　May I take your hand in mine?
Mere friends are we,—-well, friends the merest
　Keep much that I resign:

For each glance of the eye so bright and black,
　Though I keep with heart`s endeavour,—-
Your voice, when you wish the snowdrops back,
　Though it stay in my soul for ever!—-

Yet I will but say what mere friends say,
　Or only a thought stronger;
I will hold your hand but as long as all may,
　Or so very little longer!

EARTH`S IMMORTALITIES

FAME

See, as the prettiest graves will do in time,
Our poet`s wants the freshness of its prime;
Spite of the sexton`s browsing horse, the sods
Have struggled through its binding osier rods;
Headstone and half-sunk footstone lean awry,
Wanting the brick-work promised by-and-by;
How the minute grey lichens, plate o`er plate,
Have softened down the crisp-cut name and date!

LOVE

So, the year`s done with
  (*Love me for ever!*)
All March begun with,
  April`s endeavour;
May-wreaths that bound me
  June needs must sever;
Now snows fall round me,
  Quenching June`s fever—-
  (*Love me for ever!*)

MEETING AT NIGHT

The grey sea and the long black land;
And the yellow half-moon large and low;
And the startled little waves that leap
In fiery ringlets from their sleep,
As I gain the cove with pushing prow,
And quench its speed i` the slushy sand.

Then a mile of warm sea-scented beach;
Three fields to cross till a farm appears;
A tap at the pane, the quick sharp scratch
And blue spurt of a lighted match,
And a voice less loud, thro` its joys and fears,
Than the two hearts beating each to each!

PARTING AT MORNING

Round the cape of a sudden came the sea,
And the sun looked over the mountain`s rim:
And straight was a path of gold for him,
And the need of a world of men for me.

SONG

Nay but you, who do not love her,
  Is she not pure gold, my mistress?
Holds earth aught—-speak truth—-above her?
  Aught like this tress, see, and this tress,
And this last fairest tress of all,
  So fair, see, ere I let it fall?

Because, you spend your lives in praising;
  To praise, you search the wide world over:
Then why not witness, calmly gazing,
  If earth holds aught—-speak truth—-above her?
Above this tress, and this, I touch
  But cannot praise, I love so much!

A WOMAN`S LAST WORD

Let`s contend no more, Love,
  Strive nor weep:
All be as before, Love,
  —-Only sleep!

What so wild as words are?
  I and thou
In debate, as birds are,
  Hawk on bough!

See the creature stalking
  While we speak!
Hush and hide the talking,
  Cheek on cheek!

What so false as truth is,
  False to thee?
Where the serpent`s tooth is
  Shun the tree—-

Where the apple reddens
  Never pry—-
Lest we lose our Edens,
  Eve and I.

Be a god and hold me
  With a charm!
Be a man and fold me
  With thine arm!

Teach me, only teach, Love
  As I ought
I will speak thy speech, Love,
  Think thy thought—-

Meet, if thou require it,
  Both demands,
Laying flesh and spirit
  In thy hands.

That shall be to-morrow
  Not to-night:
I must bury sorrow
  Out of sight:

—-Must a little weep, Love,
  (Foolish me!)
And so fall asleep, Love,
  Loved by thee.

EVELYN HOPE

Beautiful Evelyn Hope is dead!
  Sit and watch by her side an hour.
That is her book-shelf, this her bed;
  She plucked that piece of geranium-flower,
Beginning to die too, in the glass;
  Little has yet been changed, I think:
The shutters are shut, no light may pass
Save two long rays thro` the hinge`s chink.

Sixteen years old, when she died!
  Perhaps she had scarcely heard my name;
It was not her time to love; beside,
  Her life had many a hope and aim,
Duties enough and little cares,
  And now was quiet, now astir,
Till God`s hand beckoned unawares, —-
  And the sweet white brow is all of her.

Is it too late then, Evelyn Hope?
  What, your soul was pure and true,
The good stars met in your horoscope,
  Made you of spirit, fire and dew —-
And, just because I was thrice as old
  And our paths in the world diverged so wide,
Each was nought to each, must I be told?
  We were fellow mortals, nought beside?

No, indeed! for God above
  Is great to grant, as mighty to make,
And creates the love to reward the love:
  I claim you still, for my own love`s sake!
Delayed it may be for more lives yet,
  Through worlds I shall traverse, not a few:

Much is to learn, much to forget
  Ere the time be come for taking you.

But the time will come,—-at last it will,
  When, Evelyn Hope, what meant (I shall say)
In the lower earth, in the years long still,
  That body and soul so pure and gay?
Why your hair was amber, I shall divine,
  And your mouth of your own geranium's red—-
And what you would do with me, in fine,
  In the new life come in the old one's stead.

I have lived (I shall say) so much since then,
  Given up myself so many times,
Gained me the gains of various men,
  Ransacked the ages, spoiled the climes;
Yet one thing, one, in my soul's full scope,
  Either I missed or itself missed me:
And I want and find you, Evelyn Hope!
  What is the issue? let us see!

I loved you, Evelyn, all the while.
  My heart seemed full as it could hold?
There was place and to spare for the frank young smile,
  And the red young mouth, and the hair's young gold.
So, hush,—-I will give you this leaf to keep:
  See, I shut it inside the sweet cold hand!
There, that is our secret: go to sleep!
  You will wake, and remember, and understand.

LOVE AMONG THE RUINS

Where the quiet-coloured end of evening smiles,
    Miles and miles
On the solitary pastures where our sheep
    Half-asleep
Tinkle homeward thro` the twilight, stray or stop
    As they crop—-
Was the site once of a city great and gay,
    (So they say)
Of our country`s very capital, its prince
    Ages since
Held his court in, gathered councils, wielding far
    Peace or war.

Now,—-the country does not even boast a tree,
    As you see,
To distinguish slopes of verdure, certain rills
    From the hills
Intersect and give a name to, (else they run
    Into one)
Where the domed and daring palace shot its spires
    Up like fires
O`er the hundred-gated circuit of a wall
    Bounding all,
Made of marble, men might march on nor be pressed,
    Twelve abreast.

And such plenty and perfection, see, of grass
    Never was!
Such a carpet as, this summer-time, o`erspreads
    And embeds
Every vestige of the city, guessed alone,
    Stock or stone—-
Where a multitude of men breathed joy and woe
    Long ago;

Lust of glory pricked their hearts up, dread of shame
    Struck them tame;
And that glory and that shame alike, the gold
    Bought and sold.

Now,—-the single little turret that remains
    On the plains,
By the caper overrooted, by the gourd
    Overscored,
While the patching houseleek`s head of blossom winks
    Through the chinks—-
Marks the basement whence a tower in ancient time
    Sprang sublime,
And a burning ring, all round, the chariots traced
    As they raced,
And the monarch and his minions and his dames
    Viewed the games.

And I know, while thus the quiet-coloured eve
    Smiles to leave
To their folding, all our many-tinkling fleece
    In such peace,
And the slopes and rills in undistinguished grey
    Melt away—-
That a girl with eager eyes and yellow hair
    Waits me there
In the turret whence the charioteers caught soul
    For the goal,
When the king looked, where she looks now, breathless, dumb
    Till I come.

But he looked upon the city, every side,
    Far and wide,
All the mountains topped with temples, all the glades`
    Colonnades,
All the causeys, bridges, aqueducts,—-and then,
    All the men!

When I do come, she will speak not, she will stand,
    Either hand
On my shoulder, give her eyes the first embrace
    Of my face,
Ere we rush, ere we extinguish sight and speech
    Each on each.

In one year they sent a million fighters forth
    South and North,
And they built their gods a brazen pillar high
    As the sky,
Yet reserved a thousand chariots in full force—-
    Gold, of course.
Oh heart! oh blood that freezes, blood that burns!
    Earth's returns
For whole centuries of folly, noise and sin!
    Shut them in,
With their triumphs and their glories and the rest!
    Love is best.

A LOVERS` QUARREL

Oh, what a dawn of day!
 How the March sun feels like May!
    All is blue again
    After last night`s rain,
 And the South dries the hawthorn-spray.
    Only, my Love`s away!
 I`d as lief that the blue were grey,

Runnels, which rillets swell,
Must be dancing down the dell,
    With a foaming head
    On the beryl bed
Paven smooth as a hermit`s cell;
    Each with a tale to tell,
Could my Love but attend as well.

Dearest, three months ago!
When we lived blocked-up with snow,—-
    When the wind would edge
    In and in his wedge,
In, as far as the point could go—-
    Not to our ingle, though,
Where we loved each the other so!

Laughs with so little cause!
We devised games out of straws.
    We would try and trace
    One another`s face
In the ash, as an artist draws;
    Free on each other`s flaws,
How we chattered like two church daws!

What`s in the `Times``?—-a scold
At the Emperor deep and cold;

37

He has taken a bride
To his gruesome side,
That's as fair as himself is bold:
    There they sit ermine-stoled,
And she powders her hair with gold.

Fancy the Pampas' sheen!
Miles and miles of gold and green
    Where the sunflowers blow
    In a solid glow,
And—-to break now and then the screen—-
    Black neck and eyeballs keen,
Up a wild horse leaps between!

Try, will our table turn?
Lay your hands there light, and yearn
    Till the yearning slips
    Thro' the finger-tips
In a fire which a few discern,
    And a very few feel burn,
And the rest, they may live and learn!

Then we would up and pace,
For a change, about the place,
    Each with arm o'er neck:
    'Tis our quarter-deck,
We are seamen in woeful case.
    Help in the ocean-space!
Or, if no help, we'll embrace.

See, how she looks now, dressed
In a sledging-cap and vest!
    'Tis a huge fur cloak—-
    Like a reindeer's yoke
Falls the lappet along the breast:
    Sleeves for her arms to rest,
Or to hang, as my Love likes best.

Teach me to flirt a fan
As the Spanish ladies can,
　　Or I tint your lip
　　With a burnt stick's tip
And you turn into such a man!
　　Just the two spots that span
Half the bill of the young male swan.

Dearest, three months ago
When the mesmerizer Snow
　　With his hand's first sweep
　　Put the earth to sleep:
'Twas a time when the heart could show
All—-how was earth to know,
　　'Neath the mute hand's to-and-fro?

Dearest, three months ago
When we loved each other so,
　　Lived and loved the same
　　Till an evening came
When a shaft from the devil's bow
　　Pierced to our ingle-glow,
And the friends were friend and foe!

Not from the heart beneath—-
'Twas a bubble born of breath,
　　Neither sneer nor vaunt,
　　Nor reproach nor taunt.
See a word, how it severeth!
　　Oh, power of life and death
In the tongue, as the Preacher saith!

Woman, and will you cast
For a word, quite off at last
　　Me, your own, your You,—-
　　Since, as truth is true,
I was You all the happy past—-

Me do you leave aghast
With the memories We amassed?

Love, if you knew the light
That your soul casts in my sight,
    How I look to you
    For the pure and true
And the beauteous and the right, —-
    Bear with a moment`s spite
When a mere mote threats the white!

What of a hasty word?
Is the fleshly heart not stirred
    By a worm`s pin-prick
    Where its roots are quick?
See the eye, by a fly`s foot blurred —-
    Ear, when a straw is heard
Scratch the brain`s coat of curd!

Foul be the world or fair
More or less, how can I care?
    `Tis the world the same
    For my praise or blame,
And endurance is easy there.
    Wrong in the one thing rare —-
Oh, it is hard to bear!

Here`s the spring back or close,
When the almond-blossom blows:
    We shall have the word
    In a minor third
There is none but the cuckoo knows:
    Heaps of the guelder-rose!
I must bear with it, I suppose.

Could but November come,
Were the noisy birds struck dumb
    At the warning slash

Of his driver`s-lash—-
I would laugh like the valiant Thumb
   Facing the castle glum
And the giant`s fee-faw-fum!

Then, were the world well stripped
Of the gear wherein equipped
   We can stand apart,
   Heart dispense with heart
In the sun, with the flowers unnipped,—-
   Oh, the world`s hangings ripped,
We were both in a bare-walled crypt!

Each in the crypt would cry
``But one freezes here! and why?
   ``When a heart, as chill,
   ``At my own would thrill
``Back to life, and its fires out-fly?
   ``Heart, shall we live or die?
``The rest. . . . settle by-and-by!``

So, she`d efface the score,
And forgive me as before.
   It is twelve o`clock:
   I shall hear her knock
In the worst of a storm`s uproar,
   I shall pull her through the door,
I shall have her for evermore!

UP AT A VILLA—-DOWN IN THE CITY

AS DISTINGUISHED BY AN ITALIAN PERSON OF QUALITY

Had I but plenty of money, money enough and to spare,
The house for me, no doubt, were a house in the city-square;
Ah, such a life, such a life, as one leads at the window there!

Something to see, by Bacchus, something to hear, at least!
There, the whole day long, one`s life is a perfect feast;
While up at a villa one lives, I maintain it, no more than a beast.

Well now, look at our villa! stuck like the horn of a bull
Just on a mountain-edge as bare as the creature`s skull,
Save a mere shag of a bush with hardly a leaf to pull!
—-I scratch my own, sometimes, to see if the hair`s turned wool.

But the city, oh the city—-the square with the houses! Why?
They are stone-faced, white as a curd, there`s something to take the eye!
Houses in four straight lines, not a single front awry;
You watch who crosses and gossips, who saunters, who hurries by;
Green blinds, as a matter of course, to draw when the sun gets high;
And the shops with fanciful signs which are painted properly.

What of a villa? Though winter be over in March by rights,
`Tis May perhaps ere the snow shall have withered well off the heights:
You`ve the brown ploughed land before, where the oxen steam and wheeze,
And the hills over-smoked behind by the faint grey olive-trees.

Is it better in May, I ask you? You`ve summer all at once;
In a day he leaps complete with a few strong April suns.
`Mid the sharp short emerald wheat, scarce risen three fingers well,
The wild tulip, at end of its tube, blows out its great red bell
Like a thin clear bubble of blood, for the children to pick and sell.

Is it ever hot in the square? There`s a fountain to spout and splash!
In the shade it sings and springs; in the shine such foam-bows flash
On the horses with curling fish-tails, that prance and paddle and pash
Round the lady atop in her conch—-fifty gazers do not abash,
Though all that she wears is some weeds round her waist in a sort of sash.

All the year at the villa, nothing to see though you linger,
Except yon cypress that points like a death`s lean lifted forefinger.
Some think fireflies pretty, when they mix i` the corn and mingle,
Or thrid the stinking hemp till the stalks of it seem a-tingle.
Late August or early September, the stunning cicala is shrill,
And the bees keep their tiresome whine round the resinous firs on the hill.
Enough of the seasons,—-I spare you the months of the fever and chill.

Ere you open your eyes in the city, the blessed church-bells begin:
No sooner the bells leave off than the diligence rattles in:
You get the pick of the news, and it costs you never a pin.
By-and-by there`s the travelling doctor gives pills, lets blood, draws teeth;
Or the Pulcinello-trumpet breaks up the market beneath.
At the post-office such a scene-picture—-the new play, piping hot!
And a notice how, only this morning, three liberal thieves were shot.
Above it, behold the Archbishop`s most fatherly of rebukes,
And beneath, with his crown and his lion, some little new law of the Duke`s!
Or a sonnet with flowery marge, to the Reverend Don So-and-so
Who is Dante, Boccaccio, Petrarca, Saint Jerome and Cicero,
``And moreover,`` (the sonnet goes rhyming,) ``the skirts of Saint
          Paul has reached,
``Having preached us those six Lent-lectures more unctuous than
          ever he preached.``
Noon strikes,—-here sweeps the procession! our Lady borne smiling
          and smart
With a pink gauze gown all spangles, and seven swords stuck in her heart!
Bang-whang-whang goes the drum, *tootle-to-tootle* the fife;
No keeping one`s haunches still: it`s the greatest pleasure in life.

But bless you, it`s dear—-it`s dear! fowls, wine, at double the rate.

They have clapped a new tax upon salt, and what oil pays passing
       the gate
It`s a horror to think of. And so, the villa for me, not the city!
Beggars can scarcely be choosers: but still—-ah, the pity, the pity!
Look, two and two go the priests, then the monks with cowls and sandals,
And the penitents dressed in white shirts, a-holding the yellow candles;
One` he carries a flag up straight, and another a cross with handles,
And the Duke`s guard brings up the rear, for the better prevention of scandals:
Bang-whang-whang goes the drum, *tootle-te-tootle* the fife.
Oh, a day in the city-square, there is no such pleasure in life!

A TOCCATA OF GALUPPI`S

Oh Galuppi, Baldassaro, this is very sad to find!
I can hardly misconceive you; it would prove me deaf and blind;
But although I take your meaning, `tis with such a heavy mind!

Here you come with all your music, and here`s all the good it brings.
What, they lived once thus at Venice where the merchants were the kings,
Where Saint Mark`s is, where the Doges used to wed the sea with rings?

Ay, because the sea`s the street there; and `tis arched by ... what you call
... Shylock`s bridge with houses on it, where they kept the carnival:
I was never out of England—-it`s as if I saw it all.

Did young people take their pleasure when the sea was warm in May?
Balls and masks begun at midnight, burning ever to mid-day,
When they made up fresh adventures for the morrow, do you say?

Was a lady such a lady, cheeks so round and lips so red,—-
On her neck the small face buoyant, like a bell-flower on its bed,
O`er the breast`s superb abundance where a man might base his head?

Well, and it was graceful of them—-they`d break talk off and afford
—-She, to bite her mask`s black velvet—-he, to finger on his sword,
While you sat and played Toccatas, stately at the clavichord?

What? Those lesser thirds so plaintive, sixths diminished, sigh on sigh,
Told them something? Those suspensions, those solutions—-``Must
      we die?``
Those commiserating sevenths—-``Life might last! we can but try!``

``Were you happy?``—-``Yes.``—-``And are you still as happy?``—-
``Yes. And you?``

—-``Then, more kisses!``—-``Did *I* stop them, when a million
      seemed so few?``
Hark, the dominant`s persistence till it must be answered to!

So, an octave struck the answer. Oh, they praised you, I dare say!
``Brave Galuppi! that was music! good alike at grave and gay!
``I can always leave off talking when I hear a master play!``

Then they left you for their pleasure: till in due time, one by one,
Some with lives that came to nothing, some with deeds as well undone,
Death stepped tacitly and took them where they never see the sun.

But when I sit down to reason, think to take my stand nor swerve,
While I triumph o`er a secret wrung from nature`s close reserve,
In you come with your cold music till I creep thro` every nerve.

Yes, you, like a ghostly cricket, creaking where a house was burned:
``Dust and ashes, dead and done with, Venice spent what Venice earned.
``The soul, doubtless, is immortal—-where a soul can be discerned.

``Yours for instance: you know physics, something of geology,
``Mathematics are your pastime; souls shall rise in their degree;
``Butterflies may dread extinction,—-you`ll not die, it cannot be!

``As for Venice and her people, merely born to bloom and drop,
``Here on earth they bore their fruitage, mirth and folly were the crop:
``What of soul was left, I wonder, when the kissing had to stop?

``Dust and ashes!`` So you creak it, and I want the heart to scold.
Dear dead women, with such hair, too—-what`s become of all the gold
Used to hang and brush their bosoms? I feel chilly and grown old.

OLD PICTURES IN FLORENCE

The morn when first it thunders in March,
  The eel in the pond gives a leap, they say:
As I leaned and looked over the aloed arch
  Of the villa-gate this warm March day,
No flash snapped, no dumb thunder rolled
  In the valley beneath where, white and wide
And washed by the morning water-gold,
  Florence lay out on the mountain-side.

River and bridge and street and square
  Lay mine, as much at my beck and call,
Through the live translucent bath of air,
  As the sights in a magic crystal ball.
And of all I saw and of all I praised,
  The most to praise and the best to see
Was the startling bell-tower Giotto raised:
  But why did it more than startle me?

Giotto, how, with that soul of yours,
  Could you play me false who loved you so?
Some slights if a certain heart endures
  Yet it feels, I would have your fellows know!
I` faith, I perceive not why I should care
  To break a silence that suits them best,
But the thing grows somewhat hard to bear
  When I find a Giotto join the rest.

On the arch where olives overhead
  Print the blue sky with twig and leaf,
(That sharp-curled leaf which they never shed)
  `Twixt the aloes, I used to lean in chief,
And mark through the winter afternoons,
  By a gift God grants me now and then,

In the mild decline of those suns like moons,
  Who walked in Florence, besides her men.

They might chirp and chaffer, come and go
  For pleasure or profit, her men alive—-
My business was hardly with them, I trow,
  But with empty cells of the human hive;
—-With the chapter-room, the cloister-porch,
  The church`s apsis, aisle or nave,
Its crypt, one fingers along with a torch,
  Its face set full for the sun to shave.

Wherever a fresco peels and drops,
  Wherever an outline weakens and wanes
Till the latest life in the painting stops,
  Stands One whom each fainter pulse-tick pains:
One, wishful each scrap should clutch the brick,
  Each tinge not wholly escape the plaster,
—-A lion who dies of an ass`s kick,
  The wronged great soul of an ancient Master.

For oh, this world and the wrong it does
  They are safe in heaven with their backs to it,
The Michaels and Rafaels, you hum and buzz
  Round the works of, you of the little wit!
Do their eyes contract to the earth`s old scope,
  Now that they see God face to face,
And have all attained to be poets, I hope?
  `Tis their holiday now, in any case.

Much they reck of your praise and you!
  But the wronged great souls—-can they be quit
Of a world where their work is all to do,
  Where you style them, you of the little wit,
Old Master This and Early the Other,
  Not dreaming that Old and New are fellows:
A younger succeeds to an elder brother,
  Da Vincis derive in good time from Dellos.

And here where your praise might yield returns,
  And a handsome word or two give help,
Here, after your kind, the mastiff girns
  And the puppy pack of poodles yelp.
What, not a word for Stefano there,
  Of brow once prominent and starry,
Called Nature's Ape and the world's despair
  For his peerless painting? (See Vasari.)

There stands the Master. Study, my friends,
  What a man's work comes to! So he plans it,
Performs it, perfects it, makes amends
  For the toiling and moiling, and then, *sic transit!*
Happier the thrifty blind-folk labour,
  With upturned eye while the hand is busy,
Not sidling a glance at the coin of their neighbour!
  'Tis looking downward that makes one dizzy.

``If you knew their work you would deal your dole.``
  May I take upon me to instruct you?
When Greek Art ran and reached the goal,
  Thus much had the world to boast *in fructu*—-
The Truth of Man, as by God first spoken,
  Which the actual generations garble,
Was re-uttered, and Soul (which Limbs betoken)
  And Limbs (Soul informs) made new in marble.

So, you saw yourself as you wished you were,
  As you might have been, as you cannot be;
Earth here, rebuked by Olympus there:
  And grew content in your poor degree
With your little power, by those statues' godhead,
  And your little scope, by their eyes' full sway,
And your little grace, by their grace embodied,
  And your little date, by their forms that stay.

You would fain be kinglier, say, than I am?
  Even so, you will not sit like Theseus.

You would prove a model? The Son of Priam
  Has yet the advantage in arms` and knees` use.
You`re wroth—-can you slay your snake like Apollo?
  You`re grieved—-still Niobe`s the grander!
You live—-there`s the Racers` frieze to follow:
  You die—-there`s the dying Alexander.

So, testing your weakness by their strength,
  Your meagre charms by their rounded beauty,
Measured by Art in your breadth and length,
  You learned—-to submit is a mortal`s duty.
—-When I say ``you`` `tis the common soul,
  The collective, I mean: the race of Man
That receives life in parts to live in a whole,
  And grow here according to God`s clear plan.

Growth came when, looking your last on them all,
  You turned your eyes inwardly one fine day
And cried with a start—-What if we so small
  Be greater and grander the while than they?
Are they perfect of lineament, perfect of stature?
  In both, of such lower types are we
Precisely because of our wider nature;
  For time, theirs—-ours, for eternity.

To-day`s brief passion limits their range;
  It seethes with the morrow for us and more.
They are perfect—-how else? they shall never change:
  We are faulty—-why not? we have time in store.
The Artificer`s hand is not arrested
  With us; we are rough-hewn, nowise polished:
They stand for our copy, and, once invested
  With all they can teach, we shall see them abolished.

`Tis a life-long toil till our lump be leaven—-
  The better! What`s come to perfection perishes.
Things learned on earth, we shall practise in heaven:
  Works done least rapidly, Art most cherishes.

Thyself shalt afford the example, Giotto!
  Thy one work, not to decrease or diminish,
Done at a stroke, was just (was it not?) ``O!``
  Thy great Campanile is still to finish.

Is it true that we are now, and shall be hereafter,
  But what and where depend on life`s minute?
Hails heavenly cheer or infernal laughter
  Our first step out of the gulf or in it?
Shall Man, such step within his endeavour,
  Man`s face, have no more play and action
Than joy which is crystallized for ever,
  Or grief, an eternal petrifaction?

On which I conclude, that the early painters,
  To cries of ``Greek Art and what more wish you?``—-
Replied, ``To become now self-acquainters,
  ``And paint man man, whatever the issue!
``Make new hopes shine through the flesh they fray,
  ``New fears aggrandize the rags and tatters:
``To bring the invisible full into play!
  ``Let the visible go to the dogs—-what matters?``

Give these, I exhort you, their guerdon and glory
  For daring so much, before they well did it.
The first of the new, in our race`s story,
  Beats the last of the old; `tis no idle quiddit.
The worthies began a revolution,
  Which if on earth you intend to acknowledge,
Why, honour them now! (ends my allocution)
  Nor confer your degree when the folk leave college.

There`s a fancy some lean to and others hate—-
  That, when this life is ended, begins
New work for the soul in another state,
  Where it strives and gets weary, loses and wins:
Where the strong and the weak, this world`s congeries,
  Repeat in large what they practised in small,

Through life after life in unlimited series;
  Only the scale's to be changed, that's all.

Yet I hardly know. When a soul has seen
  By the means of Evil that Good is best,
And, through earth and its noise, what is heaven's serene, —-
  When our faith in the same has stood the test —-
Why, the child grown man, you burn the rod,
  The uses of labour are surely done;
There remaineth a rest for the people of God:
  And I have had troubles enough, for one.

But at any rate I have loved the season
  Of Art's spring-birth so dim and dewy;
My sculptor is Nicolo<*1> the Pisan,
  My painter —-who but Cimabue?
Nor ever was man of them all indeed,
  From these to Ghiberti<*2> and Ghirlandaio,<*3>
Could say that he missed my critic-meed.
  So, now to my special grievance —-heigh ho!

Their ghosts still stand, as I said before,
  Watching each fresco flaked and rasped,
Blocked up, knocked out, or whitewashed o'er:
  —-No getting again what the church has grasped!
The works on the wall must take their chance;
  ``Works never conceded to England's thick clime!``
(I hope they prefer their inheritance
  Of a bucketful of Italian quick-lime.)

When they go at length, with such a shaking
  Of heads o'er the old delusion, sadly
Each master his way through the black streets taking,
  Where many a lost work breathes though badly —-
Why don't they bethink them of who has merited?
  Why not reveal, while their pictures dree
Such doom, how a captive might be out-ferreted?
  Why is it they never remember me?

Not that I expect the great Bigordi,
  Nor Sandro to hear me, chivalric, bellicose;
Nor the wronged Lippino;<*4> and not a word I
  Say of a scrap of Fr Angelico's:
But are you too fine, Taddeo Gaddi,<*5>
  To grant me a taste of your intonaco,<*6>
Some Jerome that seeks the heaven with a sad eye?
  Not a churlish saint, Lorenzo Monaco?

Could not the ghost with the close red cap,
  My Pollajolo,<*7> the twice a craftsman,
Save me a sample, give me the hap
  Of a muscular Christ that shows the draughtsman?
No Virgin by him the somewhat petty,
  Of finical touch and tempera<*8> crumbly —-
Could not Alesso Baldovinetti
  Contribute so much, I ask him humbly?

Margheritone of Arezzo,<*9>
  With the grave-clothes garb and swaddling barret
(Why purse up mouth and beak in a pet so,
  You bald old saturnine poll-clawed parrot?)
Not a poor glimmering Crucifixion,
  Where in the foreground kneels the donor?
If such remain, as is my conviction,
  The hoarding it does you but little honour.

They pass; for them the panels may thrill,
  The tempera grow alive and tinglish;
Their pictures are left to the mercies still
  Of dealers and stealers, Jews and the English,
Who, seeing mere money's worth in their prize,
  Will sell it to somebody calm as Zeno
At naked High Art, and in ecstasies
  Before some clay-cold vile Carlino!

No matter for these! But Giotto, you,
  Have you allowed, as the town-tongues babble it, —-

Oh, never! it shall not be counted true—-
  That a certain precious little tablet
Which Buonarroti eyed like a lover,—-
  Was buried so long in oblivion's womb
And, left for another than I to discover,
  Turns up at last! and to whom?—-to whom?

I, that have haunted the dim San Spirito,
  (Or was it rather the Ognissanti<*10>?)
Patient on altar-step planting a weary toe!
  Nay, I shall have it yet! *Detur amanti!*
My Koh-i-noor-or (if that's a platitude)
  Jewel of Giamschid, the Persian Sofi's eye
So, in anticipative gratitude,
  What if I take up my hope and prophesy?

When the hour grows ripe, and a certain dotard
  Is pitched, no parcel that needs invoicing,
To the worse side of the Mont Saint Gothard,
  We shall begin by way of rejoicing;
None of that shooting the sky (blank cartridge),
  Nor a civic guard, all plumes and lacquer,
Hunting Radetzky's soul like a partridge
  Over Morello with squib and cracker.

This time we'll shoot better game and bag 'em hot—-
  No mere display at the stone of Dante,
But a kind of sober Witanagemot
  (Ex: ``Casa Guidi,`` *quod videas ante*)
Shall ponder, once Freedom restored to Florence,
  How Art may return that departed with her.
Go, hated house, go each trace of the Loraine's,
  And bring us the days of Orgagna<*11> hither!

How we shall prologize, how we shall perorate,
  Utter fit things upon art and history,
Feel truth at blood-heat and falsehood at zero rate,
  Make of the want of the age no mystery;

Contrast the fructuous and sterile eras,
  Show — -monarchy ever its uncouth cub licks
Out of the bear's shape into Chimra's,
  While Pure Art's birth is still the republic's.

Then one shall propose in a speech (curt Tuscan,
  Expurgate and sober, with scarcely an ``issimo,``)
To end now our half-told tale of Cambuscan,<*12>
  And turn the bell-tower's *alt* to *altissimo*:
And fine as the beak of a young beccaccia<*13>
  The Campanile, the Duomo's fit ally,
Shall soar up in gold full fifty braccia,
  Completing Florence, as Florence Italy.

Shall I be alive that morning the scaffold
  Is broken away, and the long-pent fire,
Like the golden hope of the world, unbaffled
  Springs from its sleep, and up goes the spire
While ``God and the People`` plain for its motto,
  Thence the new tricolour flaps at the sky?
At least to foresee that glory of Giotto
  And Florence together, the first am I!

* 1 A sculptor, died 1278.
* 2 Died 1455. Designed the bronze gates of the Baptistry at Florence.
* 3 A painter, died 1498.
* 4 The son of Fr Lippo Lippi. Wronged, because some of his
* pictures have been attributed to others.
* 5 Died 1366. One of Giotto's pupils and assistants.
* 6 Rough cast.
* 7 Painter, sculptor, and goldsmith.
* 8 Distemper — -mixture of water and egg yolk.
* 9 Sculptor and architect, died 1313-
*10 All Saints.
*11 A Florentine painter, died 1576.
*12 Tartar king.
*13 A woodcock

``DE GUSTIBUS—-``

Your ghost will walk, you lover of trees,
  (If our loves remain)
  In an English lane,
By a cornfield-side a-flutter with poppies.
Hark, those two in the hazel coppice—-
A boy and a girl, if the good fates please,
  Making love, say,—-
  The happier they!
Draw yourself up from the light of the moon,
And let them pass, as they will too soon,
  With the bean-flowers` boon,
  And the blackbird`s tune,
  And May, and June!

What I love best in all the world
Is a castle, precipice-encurled,
In a gash of the wind-grieved Apennine
Or look for me, old fellow of mine,
(If I get my head from out the mouth
O` the grave, and loose my spirit`s bands,
And come again to the land of lands)—-
In a sea-side house to the farther South,
Where the baked cicala dies of drouth,
And one sharp tree—-`tis a cypress—-stands,
By the many hundred years red-rusted,
Rough iron-spiked, ripe fruit-o`ercrusted,
My sentinel to guard the sands
To the water`s edge. For, what expands
Before the house, but the great opaque
Blue breadth of sea without a break?
While, in the house, for ever crumbles
Some fragment of the frescoed walls,
From blisters where a scorpion sprawls.
A girl bare-footed brings, and tumbles

Down on the pavement, green-flesh melons,
And says there`s news to-day—-the king
Was shot at, touched in the liver-wing,
Goes with his Bourbon arm in a sling:
—-She hopes they have not caught the felons.
Italy, my Italy!
Queen Mary`s saying serves for me—-
    (When fortune`s malice
    Lost her—-Calais)—-
Open my heart and you will see
Graved inside of it, ``Italy.``
Such lovers old are I and she:
So it always was, so shall ever be!

HOME-THOUGHTS, FROM ABROAD

Oh, to be in England
Now that April's there,
And whoever wakes in England
Sees, some morning, unaware,
That the lowest boughs and the brushwood sheaf
Round the elm-tree bole are in tiny leaf,
While the chaffinch sings on the orchard bough
In England—-now!!

And after April, when May follows,
And the whitethroat builds, and all the swallows!
Hark, where my blossomed pear-tree in the hedge
Leans to the field and scatters on the clover
Blossoms and dewdrops—-at the bent spray's edge—-
That's the wise thrush; he sings each song twice over,
Lest you should think he never could recapture
The first fine careless rapture!
And though the fields look rough with hoary dew,
All will be gay when noontide wakes anew
The buttercups, the little children's dower
—-Far brighter than this gaudy melon-flower

HOME-THOUGHTS, FROM THE SEA

Nobly, nobly Cape Saint Vincent to the North-west died away;
Sunset ran, one glorious blood-red, reeking into Cadiz Bay;
Bluish `mid the burning water, full in face Trafalgar lay;
In the dimmest North-east distance dawned Gibraltar grand and gray;
``Here and here did England help me: how can I help England?``—-say,
Whoso turns as I, this evening, turn to God to praise and pray,
While Jove`s planet rises yonder, silent over Africa.

SAUL

Said Abner, ``At last thou art come! Ere I tell, ere thou speak,
``Kiss my cheek, wish me well!`` Then I wished it, and did kiss his cheek.
And he, ``Since the King, O my friend, for thy countenance sent,
``Neither drunken nor eaten have we; nor until from his tent
``Thou return with the joyful assurance the King liveth yet,
``Shall our lip with the honey be bright, with the water be wet.
``For out of the black mid-tent`s silence, a space of three days,
``Not a sound hath escaped to thy servants, of prayer nor of praise,
``To betoken that Saul and the Spirit have ended their strife,
``And that, faint in his triumph, the monarch sinks back upon life.

``Yet now my heart leaps, O beloved! God`s child with his dew
``On thy gracious gold hair, and those lilies still living and blue
``Just broken to twine round thy harp-strings, as if no wild beat
``Were now raging to torture the desert!``

Then I, as was meet,
Knelt down to the God of my fathers, and rose on my feet,
And ran o`er the sand burnt to powder. The tent was unlooped;
I pulled up the spear that obstructed, and under I stooped
Hands and knees on the slippery grass-patch, all withered and gone,
That extends to the second enclosure, I groped my way on
Till I felt where the foldskirts fly open. Then once more I prayed,
And opened the foldskirts and entered, and was not afraid
But spoke, ``Here is David, thy servant!`` And no voice replied.
At the first I saw nought but the blackness but soon I descried
A something more black than the blackness—-the vast, the upright
Main prop which sustains the pavilion: and slow into sight
Grew a figure against it, gigantic and blackest of all.
Then a sunbeam, that burst thro` the tent-roof, showed Saul.

He stood as erect as that tent-prop, both arms stretched out wide
On the great cross-support in the centre, that goes to each side;

He relaxed not a muscle, but hung there as, caught in his pangs
And waiting his change, the king-serpent all heavily hangs,
Far away from his kind, in the pine, till deliverance come
With the spring-time,—-so agonized Saul, drear and stark, blind and dumb.

Then I tuned my harp,—-took off the lilies we twine round its chords
Lest they snap 'neath the stress of the noon-tide—-those sunbeams
      like swords!
And I first played the tune all our sheep know, as, one after one,
So docile they come to the pen-door till folding be done.
They are white and untorn by the bushes, for lo, they have fed
Where the long grasses stifle the water within the stream's bed;
And now one after one seeks its lodging, as star follows star
Into eve and the blue far above us,—-so blue and so far!

—-Then the tune, for which quails on the cornland will each leave his
mate
To fly after the player; then, what makes the crickets elate
Till for boldness they fight one another: and then, what has weight
To set the quick jerboa<*1> amusing outside his sand house—-
There are none such as he for a wonder, half bird and half mouse!
God made all the creatures and gave them our love and our fear,
To give sign, we and they are his children, one family here.

Then I played the help-tune of our reapers, their wine-song, when hand
Grasps at hand, eye lights eye in good friendship, and great hearts expand
And grow one in the sense of this world's life.—-And then, the last song
When the dead man is praised on his journey—-``Bear, bear him along
``With his few faults shut up like dead flowerets! Are balm-seeds not here
``To console us? The land has none left such as he on the bier.
``Oh, would we might keep thee, my brother!''—-And then, the glad
chaunt
Of the marriage,—-first go the young maidens, next, she whom we vaunt
As the beauty, the pride of our dwelling.—-And then, the great
march
Wherein man runs to man to assist him and buttress an arch

Nought can break; who shall harm them, our friends?—-Then, the
  chorus intoned
As the Levites go up to the altar in glory enthroned.
But I stopped here: for here in the darkness Saul groaned.

And I paused, held my breath in such silence, and listened apart;
And the tent shook, for mighty Saul shuddered: and sparkles `gan dart
From the jewels that woke in his turban, at once with a start,
All its lordly male-sapphires, and rubies courageous at heart.
So the head: but the body still moved not, still hung there erect.
And I bent once again to my playing, pursued it unchecked,
As I sang,—-

  ``Oh, our manhood`s prime vigour! No spirit feels waste,
``Not a muscle is stopped in its playing nor sinew unbraced.
``Oh, the wild joys of living! the leaping from rock up to rock,
``The strong rending of boughs from the fir-tree, the cool silver shock
``Of the plunge in a pool`s living water, the hunt of the bear,
``And the sultriness showing the lion is couched in his lair.
``And the meal, the rich dates yellowed over with gold dust divine,
``And the locust-flesh steeped in the pitcher, the full draught of wine,
``And the sleep in the dried river-channel where bulrushes tell
``That the water was wont to go warbling so softly and well.
``How good is man`s life, the mere living! how fit to employ
``All the heart and the soul and the senses for ever in joy!
``Hast thou loved the white locks of thy father, whose sword thou
  didst guard
``When he trusted thee forth with the armies, for glorious reward?
``Didst thou see the thin hands of thy mother, held up as men sung
``The low song of the nearly-departed, and bear her faint tongue
``Joining in while it could to the witness, `Let one more attest,
`` `I have lived, seen God`s hand thro`a lifetime, and all was for best`?
``Then they sung thro` their tears in strong triumph, not much, but
  the rest.
``And thy brothers, the help and the contest, the working whence grew
``Such result as, from seething grape-bundles, the spirit strained true:
``And the friends of thy boyhood—-that boyhood of wonder and hope,
``Present promise and wealth of the future beyond the eye`s scope,—-

``Till lo, thou art grown to a monarch; a people is thine;
``And all gifts, which the world offers singly, on one head combine!
``On one head, all the beauty and strength, love and rage (like the throe
``That, a-work in the rock, helps its labour and lets the gold go)
``High ambition and deeds which surpass it, fame crowning them,—-all
``Brought to blaze on the head of one creature—-King Saul!``

And lo, with that leap of my spirit,—-heart, hand, harp and voice,
Each lifting Saul`s name out of sorrow, each bidding rejoice
Saul`s fame in the light it was made for—-as when, dare I say,
The Lord`s army, in rapture of service, strains through its array,
And up soareth the cherubim-chariot—-``Saul!`` cried I, and
stopped,
And waited the thing that should follow. Then Saul, who hung propped
By the tent`s cross-support in the centre, was struck by his name.
Have ye seen when Spring`s arrowy summons goes right to the aim,
And some mountain, the last to withstand her, that held (he alone,
While the vale laughed in freedom and flowers) on a broad bust of stone
A year`s snow bound about for a breastplate,—-leaves grasp of the sheet?
Fold on fold all at once it crowds thunderously down to his feet,
And there fronts you, stark, black, but alive yet, your mountain of old,
With his rents, the successive bequeathings of ages untold—-
Yea, each harm got in fighting your battles, each furrow and scar
Of his head thrust `twixt you and the tempest—-all hail, there they are!
—-Now again to be softened with verdure, again hold the nest
Of the dove, tempt the goat and its young to the green on his crest
For their food in the ardours of summer. One long shudder thrilled
All the tent till the very air tingled, then sank and was stilled
At the King`s self left standing before me, released and aware.
What was gone, what remained? All to traverse, `twixt hope and despair;
Death was past, life not come: so he waited. Awhile his right hand
Held the brow, helped the eyes left too vacant forthwith to remand
To their place what new objects should enter: `twas Saul as before.
I looked up and dared gaze at those eyes, nor was hurt any more
Than by slow pallid sunsets in autumn, ye watch from the shore,
At their sad level gaze o`er the ocean—-a sun`s slow decline
Over hills which, resolved in stern silence, o`erlap and entwine

Base with base to knit strength more intensely: so, arm folded arm
O`er the chest whose slow heavings subsided.

    What spell or what charm,
(For, awhile there was trouble within me) what next should I urge
To sustain him where song had restored him?—-Song filled to the verge
His cup with the wine of this life, pressing all that it yields
Of mere fruitage, the strength and the beauty: beyond, on what fields,
Glean a vintage more potent and perfect to brighten the eye
And bring blood to the lip, and commend them the cup they put by?
He saith, ``It is good;`` still he drinks not: he lets me praise life,
Gives assent, yet would die for his own part.

    Then fancies grew rife
Which had come long ago on the pasture, when round me the sheep
Fed in silence—-above, the one eagle wheeled slow as in sleep;
And I lay in my hollow and mused on the world that might lie
`Neath his ken, though I saw but the strip `twixt the hill and the sky:
And I laughed—-``Since my days are ordained to be passed with my flocks,
``Let me people at least, with my fancies, the plains and the rocks,
``Dream the life I am never to mix with, and image the show
``Of mankind as they live in those fashions I hardly shall know!
``Schemes of life, its best rules and right uses, the courage that gains,
``And the prudence that keeps what men strive for.`` And now these
         old trains
Of vague thought came again; I grew surer; so, once more the string
Of my harp made response to my spirit, as thus—-
    ``Yea, my King,``
I began—-``thou dost well in rejecting mere comforts that spring
``From the mere mortal life held in common by man and by brute:
``In our flesh grows the branch of this life, in our soul it bears fruit.
``Thou hast marked the slow rise of the tree,—-how its stem trembled first
``Till it passed the kid`s lip, the stag`s antler then safely outburst
``The fan-branches all round; and thou mindest when these too, in turn
``Broke a-bloom and the palm-tree seemed perfect: yet more was to learn,
``E`en the good that comes in with the palm-fruit. Our dates shall we slight,
``When their juice brings a cure for all sorrow? or care for the plight

``Of the palm`s self whose slow growth produced them? Not so!
    stem and branch
``Shall decay, nor be known in their place, while the palm-wine shall staunch
``Every wound of man`s spirit in winter. I pour thee such wine.
``Leave the flesh to the fate it was fit for! the spirit be thine!
``By the spirit, when age shall o`ercome thee, thou still shalt enjoy
``More indeed, than at first when inconscious, the life of a boy.
``Crush that life, and behold its wine running! Each deed thou hast done
``Dies, revives, goes to work in the world; until e`en as the sun
``Looking down on the earth, though clouds spoil him, though
    tempests efface,
``Can find nothing his own deed produced not, must everywhere trace
``The results of his past summer-prime`—-so, each ray of thy will,
``Every flash of thy passion and prowess, long over, shall thrill
``Thy whole people, the countless, with ardour, till they too give forth
``A like cheer to their sons, who in turn, fill the South and the North
``With the radiance thy deed was the germ of. Carouse in the past!
``But the license of age has its limit; thou diest at last:
``As the lion when age dims his eyeball, the rose at her height
``So with man—-so his power and his beauty for ever take flight.
``No! Again a long draught of my soul-wine! Look forth o`er the years!
``Thou hast done now with eyes for the actual; begin with the seer`s!
``Is Saul dead? In the depth of the vale make his tomb—-bid arise
``A grey mountain of marble heaped four-square, till, built to the skies,
``Let it mark where the great First King slumbers: whose fame would
    ye know?
``Up above see the rock`s naked face, where the record shall go
``In great characters cut by the scribe,—-Such was Saul, so he did;
``With the sages directing the work, by the populace chid,—-
``For not half, they`ll affirm, is comprised there! Which fault to amend,
``In the grove with his kind grows the cedar, whereon they shall spend
``(See, in tablets `tis level before them) their praise, and record
``With the gold of the graver, Saul`s story,—-the statesman`s great word
``Side by side with the poet`s sweet comment. The river`s a-wave
``With smooth paper-reeds grazing each other when prophet-winds rave:
``So the pen gives unborn generations their due and their part
``In thy being! Then, first of the mighty, thank God that thou art!``

And behold while I sang ... but O Thou who didst grant me that day,
And before it not seldom hast granted thy help to essay,
Carry on and complete an adventure,—-my shield and my sword
In that act where my soul was thy servant, thy word was my word,—-
Still be with me, who then at the summit of human endeavour
And scaling the highest, man`s thought could, gazed hopeless as ever
On the new stretch of heaven above me—-till, mighty to save,

Just one lift of thy hand cleared that distance—-God`s throne from
        man`s grave!
Let me tell out my tale to its ending—-my voice to my heart
Which can scarce dare believe in what marvels last night I took part,
As this morning I gather the fragments, alone with my sheep,
And still fear lest the terrible glory evanish like sleep!
For I wake in the grey dewy covert, while Hebron<*2> upheaves
The dawn struggling with night on his shoulder, and Kidron<*3> retrieves
Slow the damage of yesterday`s sunshine.

        I say then,—-my song
While I sang thus, assuring the monarch, and ever more strong
Made a proffer of good to console him—-he slowly resumed
His old motions and habitudes kingly. The right-hand replumed
His black locks to their wonted composure, adjusted the swathes
Of his turban, and see—-the huge sweat that his countenance bathes,
He wipes off with the robe; and he girds now his loins as of yore,
And feels slow for the armlets of price, with the clasp set before.
He is Saul, ye remember in glory,—-ere error had bent
The broad brow from the daily communion; and still, though much spent
Be the life and the bearing that front you, the same, God did choose,
To receive what a man may waste, desecrate, never quite lose.
So sank he along by the tent-prop till, stayed by the pile
Of his armour and war-cloak and garments, he leaned there awhile,
And sat out my singing,—-one arm round the tent-prop, to raise
His bent head, and the other hung slack—-till I touched on the praise
I foresaw from all men in all time, to the man patient there;
And thus ended, the harp falling forward. Then first I was `ware
That he sat, as I say, with my head just above his vast knees
Which were thrust out on each side around me, like oak-roots which please

66

To encircle a lamb when it slumbers. I looked up to know
If the best I could do had brought solace: he spoke not, but slow
Lifted up the hand slack at his side, till he laid it with care
Soft and grave, but in mild settled will, on my brow: thro` my hair
The large fingers were pushed, and he bent back my bead, with kind power—-
All my face back, intent to peruse it, as men do a flower.
Thus held he me there with his great eyes that scrutinized mine—-
And oh, all my heart how it loved him! but where was the sign?
I yearned—-``Could I help thee, my father, inventing a bliss,
``I would add, to that life of the past, both the future and this;
``I would give thee new life altogether, as good, ages hence,
``As this moment,—-had love but the warrant, love`s heart to
dispense!``

Then the truth came upon me. No harp more—-no song more!
outbroke—-

``I have gone the whole round of creation: I saw and I spoke:
``I, a work of God`s hand for that purpose, received in my brain
``And pronounced on the rest of his hand-work—-returned him again
``His creation`s approval or censure: I spoke as I saw:
``I report, as a man may of God`s work—-all`s love, yet all`s law.
``Now I lay down the judgeship he lent me. Each faculty tasked
``To perceive him, has gained an abyss, where a dewdrop was asked.
``Have I knowledge? confounded it shrivels at Wisdom laid bare.
``Have I forethought? how purblind, how blank, to the Infinite Care!
``Do I task any faculty highest, to image success?
``I but open my eyes,—-and perfection, no more and no less,
``In the kind I imagined, full-fronts me, and God is seen God
``In the star, in the stone, in the flesh, in the soul and the clod.
``And thus looking within and around me, I ever renew
``(With that stoop of the soul which in bending upraises it too)
``The submission of man`s nothing-perfect to God`s all-complete,
``As by each new obeisance in spirit, I climb to his feet.
``Yet with all this abounding experience, this deity known,
``I shall dare to discover some province, some gift of my own.
``There`s a faculty pleasant to exercise, hard to hoodwink,
``I am fain to keep still in abeyance, (I laugh as I think)

``Lest, insisting to claim and parade in it, wot ye, I worst
``E`en the Giver in one gift.—-Behold, I could love if I durst!
``But I sink the pretension as fearing a man may o`ertake
``God`s own speed in the one way of love: I abstain for love`s sake.
``—-What, my soul? see thus far and no farther? when doors great
       and small,
``Nine-and-ninety flew ope at our touch, should the hundredth appal?
``In the least things have faith, yet distrust in the greatest of all?
``Do I find love so full in my nature, God`s ultimate gift,
``That I doubt his own love can compete with it? Here, the parts shift?
``Here, the creature surpass the Creator,—-the end, what Began?
``Would I fain in my impotent yearning do all for this man,
``And dare doubt he alone shall not help him, who yet alone can?
``Would it ever have entered my mind, the bare will, much less power,
``To bestow on this Saul what I sang of, the marvellous dower
``Of the life he was gifted and filled with? to make such a soul,
``Such a body, and then such an earth for insphering the whole?
``And doth it not enter my mind (as my warm tears attest)
``These good things being given, to go on, and give one more, the best?
``Ay, to save and redeem and restore him, maintain at the height
``This perfection,—-succeed with life`s day-spring, death`s minute of night?
``Interpose at the difficult minute, snatch Saul the mistake,
``Saul the failure, the ruin he seems now,—-and bid him awake
``From the dream, the probation, the prelude, to find himself set
``Clear and safe in new light and new life,—-a new harmony yet
``To be run, and continued, and ended—-who knows?—-or endure!
``The man taught enough, by life`s dream, of the rest to make sure;
``By the pain-throb, triumphantly winning intensified bliss,
``And the next world`s reward and repose, by the struggles in this.
``I believe it! `Tis thou, God, that givest, `tis I who receive:
``In the first is the last, in thy will is my power to believe.
``All`s one gift: thou canst grant it moreover, as prompt to my prayer
``As I breathe out this breath, as I open these arms to the air.
``From thy will, stream the worlds, life and nature, thy dread Sabaoth:
``*I* will?—-the mere atoms despise me! Why am I not loth
``To look that, even that in the face too? Why is it I dare
``Think but lightly of such impuissance? What stops my despair?

``This;—-`tis not what man Does which exalts him, but what man
         Would do!
``See the King—-I would help him but cannot, the wishes fall through.
``Could I wrestle to raise him from sorrow, grow poor to enrich,
``To fill up his life, starve my own out, I would—-knowing which,
``I know that my service is perfect. Oh, speak through me now!
``Would I suffer for him that I love? So wouldst thou—-so wilt thou!
``So shall crown thee the topmost, ineffablest, uttermost crown—-
``And thy love fill infinitude wholly, nor leave up nor down
``One spot for the creature to stand in! It is by no breath,
``Turn of eye, wave of hand, that salvation joins issue with death!
``As thy Love is discovered almighty, almighty be proved
``Thy power, that exists with and for it, of being Beloved!
``He who did most, shall bear most; the strongest shall stand the
         most weak.
```Tis the weakness in strength, that I cry for! my flesh, that I seek
``In the Godhead! I seek and I find it. O Saul, it shall be
``A Face like my face that receives thee; a Man like to me,
``Thou shalt love and be loved by, for ever: a Hand like this hand
``Shall throw open the gates of new life to thee! See the Christ stand!``

I know not too well how I found my way home in the night.
There were witnesses, cohorts about me, to left and to right,
Angels, powers, the unuttered, unseen, the alive, the aware:
I repressed, I got through them as hardly, as strugglingly there,
As a runner beset by the populace famished for news—-
Life or death. The whole earth was awakened, hell loosed with her crews;
And the stars of night beat with emotion, and tingled and shot
Out in fire the strong pain of pent knowledge: but I fainted not,
For the Hand still impelled me at once and supported, suppressed
All the tumult, and quenched it with quiet, and holy behest,
Till the rapture was shut in itself, and the earth sank to rest.
Anon at the dawn, all that trouble had withered from earth—-
Not so much, but I saw it die out in the day`s tender birth;
In the gathered intensity brought to the grey of the hills;
In the shuddering forests` held breath; in the sudden wind-thrills;
In the startled wild beasts that bore off, each with eye sidling still
Though averted with wonder and dread; in the birds stiff and chill
```

That rose heavily, as I approached them, made stupid with awe:
E`en the serpent that slid away silent,—-he felt the new law.
The same stared in the white humid faces upturned by the flowers;
The same worked in the heart of the cedar and moved the vine-bowers:
And the little brooks witnessing murmured, persistent and low,
With their obstinate, all but hushed voices—-``E`en so, it is so!``

* 1 The jumping hare.
* 2 One of the three cities of Refuge.
* 3 A brook in Jerusalem.

Dramatic Lyrics

MY STAR

All, that I know
Of a certain star
Is, it can throw
(Like the angled spar)
Now a dart of red,
Now a dart of blue
Till my friends have said
They would fain see, too,
My star that dartles the red and the blue!
Then it stops like a bird; like a flower, hangs furled:
  They must solace themselves with the Saturn above it.
What matter to me if their star is a world?
  Mine has opened its soul to me; therefore I love it.

BY THE FIRE-SIDE

How well I know what I mean to do
  When the long dark autumn-evenings come:
And where, my soul, is thy pleasant hue?
  With the music of all thy voices, dumb
In life's November too!

I shall be found by the fire, suppose,
  O'er a great wise book as beseemeth age,
While the shutters flap as the cross-wind blows
  And I turn the page, and I turn the page,
Not verse now, only prose!

Till the young ones whisper, finger on lip,
  ``There he is at it, deep in Greek:
``Now then, or never, out we slip
  ``To cut from the hazels by the creek
``A mainmast for our ship!``

I shall be at it indeed, my friends:
  Greek puts already on either side
Such a branch-work forth as soon extends
  To a vista opening far and wide,
And I pass out where it ends.

The outside-frame, like your hazel-trees:
  But the inside-archway widens fast,
And a rarer sort succeeds to these,
  And we slope to Italy at last
And youth, by green degrees.

I follow wherever I am led,
  Knowing so well the leader's hand:
Oh woman-country, wooed not wed,

Loved all the more by earth`s male-lands,
Laid to their hearts instead!

Look at the ruined chapel again
  Half-way up in the Alpine gorge!
Is that a tower, I point you plain,
  Or is it a mill, or an iron-forge
Breaks solitude in vain?

A turn, and we stand in the heart of things:
  The woods are round us, heaped and dim;
From slab to slab how it slips and springs,
  The thread of water single and slim,
Through the ravage some torrent brings!

Does it feed the little lake below?
  That speck of white just on its marge
Is Pella; see, in the evening-glow,
  How sharp the silver spear-heads charge
When Alp meets heaven in snow!

On our other side is the straight-up rock;
  And a path is kept `twixt the gorge and it
By boulder-stones where lichens mock
  The marks on a moth, and small ferns fit
Their teeth to the polished block.

Oh the sense of the yellow mountain-flowers,
  And thorny balls, each three in one,
The chestnuts throw on our path in showers!
  For the drop of the woodland fruit`s begun,
These early November hours,

That crimson the creeper`s leaf across
  Like a splash of blood, intense, abrupt,
O`er a shield else gold from rim to boss,
  And lay it for show on the fairy-cupped
Elf-needled mat of moss,

By the rose-flesh mushrooms, undivulged
  Last evening—-nay, in to-day`s first dew
Yon sudden coral nipple bulged,
  Where a freaked fawn-coloured flaky crew
Of toadstools peep indulged.

And yonder, at foot of the fronting ridge
  That takes the turn to a range beyond,
Is the chapel reached by the one-arched bridge
  Where the water is stopped in a stagnant pond
Danced over by the midge.

The chapel and bridge are of stone alike,
  Blackish-grey and mostly wet;
Cut hemp-stalks steep in the narrow dyke.
  See here again, how the lichens fret
And the roots of the ivy strike!

Poor little place, where its one priest comes
  On a festa-day, if he comes at all,
To the dozen folk from their scattered homes,
  Gathered within that precinct small
By the dozen ways one roams—-

To drop from the charcoal-burners` huts,
  Or climb from the hemp-dressers` low shed,
Leave the grange where the woodman stores his nuts,
  Or the wattled cote where the fowlers spread
Their gear on the rock`s bare juts.

It has some pretension too, this front,
  With its bit of fresco half-moon-wise
Set over the porch, Art`s early wont:
  `Tis John in the Desert, I surmise,
But has borne the weather`s brunt—-

Not from the fault of the builder, though,
  For a pent-house properly projects

Where three carved beams make a certain show,
  Dating—-good thought of our architect's—-
`Five, six, nine, he lets you know.

And all day long a bird sings there,
  And a stray sheep drinks at the pond at times;
The place is silent and aware;
  It has had its scenes, its joys and crimes,
But that is its own affair.

My perfect wife, my Leonor,
  Oh heart, my own, oh eyes, mine too,
Whom else could I dare look backward for,
  With whom beside should I dare pursue
The path grey heads abhor?

For it leads to a crag's sheer edge with them;
  Youth, flowery all the way, there stops—-
Not they; age threatens and they contemn,
  Till they reach the gulf wherein youth drops,
One inch from life's safe hem!

With me, youth led ... I will speak now,
  No longer watch you as you sit
Reading by fire-light, that great brow
  And the spirit-small hand propping it,
Mutely, my heart knows how—-

When, if I think but deep enough,
  You are wont to answer, prompt as rhyme;
And you, too, find without rebuff
  Response your soul seeks many a time
Piercing its fine flesh-stuff.

My own, confirm me! If I tread
  This path back, is it not in pride
To think how little I dreamed it led

To an age so blest that, by its side,
Youth seems the waste instead?

My own, see where the years conduct!
  At first, `twas something our two souls
Should mix as mists do; each is sucked
  In each now: on, the new stream rolls,
Whatever rocks obstruct.

Think, when our one soul understands
  The great Word which makes all things new,
When earth breaks up and heaven expands,
  How will the change strike me and you
In the house not made with hands?

Oh I must feel your brain prompt mine,
  Your heart anticipate my heart,
You must be just before, in fine,
  See and make me see, for your part,
New depths of the divine!

But who could have expected this
  When we two drew together first
Just for the obvious human bliss,
  To satisfy life`s daily thirst
With a thing men seldom miss?

Come back with me to the first of all,
  Let us lean and love it over again,
Let us now forget and now recall,
  Break the rosary in a pearly rain,
And gather what we let fall!

What did I say?—-that a small bird sings
  All day long, save when a brown pair
Of hawks from the wood float with wide wings
  Strained to a bell: `gainst noon-day glare
You count the streaks and rings.

But at afternoon or almost eve
  'Tis better; then the silence grows
To that degree, you half believe
  It must get rid of what it knows,
Its bosom does so heave.

Hither we walked then, side by side,
  Arm in arm and cheek to cheek,
And still I questioned or replied,
  While my heart, convulsed to really speak,
Lay choking in its pride.

Silent the crumbling bridge we cross,
  And pity and praise the chapel sweet,
And care about the fresco's loss,
  And wish for our souls a like retreat,
And wonder at the moss.

Stoop and kneel on the settle under,
  Look through the window's grated square:
Nothing to see! For fear of plunder,
  The cross is down and the altar bare,
As if thieves don't fear thunder.

We stoop and look in through the grate,
  See the little porch and rustic door,
Read duly the dead builder's date;
  Then cross the bridge that we crossed before,
Take the path again—-but wait!

Oh moment, one and infinite!
  The water slips o'er stock and stone;
The West is tender, hardly bright:
  How grey at once is the evening grown—-
One star, its chrysolite!

We two stood there with never a third,
  But each by each, as each knew well:

The sights we saw and the sounds we heard,
  The lights and the shades made up a spell
Till the trouble grew and stirred.

Oh, the little more, and how much it is!
  And the little less, and what worlds away!
How a sound shall quicken content to bliss,
  Or a breath suspend the blood`s best play,
And life be a proof of this!

Had she willed it, still had stood the screen
  So slight, so sure, `twixt my love and her:
I could fix her face with a guard between,
  And find her soul as when friends confer,
Friends—-lovers that might have been.

For my heart had a touch of the woodland-time,
  Wanting to sleep now over its best.
Shake the whole tree in the summer-prime,
  But bring to the Iast leaf no such test!
``Hold the last fast!`` runs the rhyme.

For a chance to make your little much,
  To gain a lover and lose a friend,
Venture the tree and a myriad such,
  When nothing you mar but the year can mend:
But a last leaf—-fear to touch!

Yet should it unfasten itself and fall
  Eddying down till it find your face
At some slight wind—-best chance of all!
  Be your heart henceforth its dwelling-place
You trembled to forestall!

Worth how well, those dark grey eyes,
  That hair so dark and dear, how worth
That a man should strive and agonize,

And taste a veriest hell on earth
For the hope of such a prize!

You might have turned and tried a man,
  Set him a space to weary and wear,
And prove which suited more your plan,
  His best of hope or his worst despair,
Yet end as he began.

But you spared me this, like the heart you are,
  And filled my empty heart at a word.
If two lives join, there is oft a scar,
  They are one and one, with a shadowy third;
One near one is too far.

A moment after, and hands unseen
  Were hanging the night around us fast
But we knew that a bar was broken between
  Life and life: we were mixed at last
In spite of the mortal screen.

The forests had done it; there they stood;
  We caught for a moment the powers at play:
They had mingled us so, for once and good,
  Their work was done—-we might go or stay,
They relapsed to their ancient mood.

How the world is made for each of us!
  How all we perceive and know in it
Tends to some moment's product thus,
  When a soul declares itself—-to wit,
By its fruit, the thing it does

Be hate that fruit or love that fruit,
  It forwards the general deed of man,
And each of the Many helps to recruit
  The life of the race by a general plan;
Each living his own, to boot.

I am named and known by that moment`s feat;
  There took my station and degree;
So grew my own small life complete,
  As nature obtained her best of me—-
One born to love you, sweet!

And to watch you sink by the fire-side now
  Back again, as you mutely sit
Musing by fire-light, that great brow
  And the spirit-small hand propping it,
Yonder, my heart knows how!

So, earth has gained by one man the more,
  And the gain of earth must be heaven`s gain too;
And the whole is well worth thinking o`er
  When autumn comes: which I mean to do
One day, as I said before.

ANY WIFE TO ANY HUSBAND

My love, this is the bitterest, that thou—-
Who art all truth, and who dost love me now
  As thine eyes say, as thy voice breaks to say—-
Shouldst love so truly, and couldst love me still
A whole long life through, had but love its will,
  Would death that leads me from thee brook delay.

I have but to be by thee, and thy hand
Will never let mine go, nor heart withstand
  The beating of my heart to reach its place.
When shall I look for thee and feel thee gone?
When cry for the old comfort and find none?
  Never, I know! Thy soul is in thy face.

Oh, I should fade—-'tis willed so! Might I save,
Gladly I would, whatever beauty gave
  Joy to thy sense, for that was precious too.
It is not to be granted. But the soul
Whence the love comes, all ravage leaves that whole;
  Vainly the flesh fades; soul makes all things new.

It would not be because my eye grew dim
Thou couldst not find the love there, thanks to Him
  Who never is dishonoured in the spark
He gave us from his fire of fires, and bade
Remember whence it sprang, nor be afraid
  While that burns on, though all the rest grow dark.

So, how thou wouldst be perfect, white and clean
Outside as inside, soul and soul's demesne
  Alike, this body given to show it by!
Oh, three-parts through the worst of life's abyss,
What plaudits from the next world after this,
  Couldst thou repeat a stroke and gain the sky!

And is it not the bitterer to think
That, disengage our hands and thou wilt sink
  Although thy love was love in very deed?
I know that nature! Pass a festive day,
Thou dost not throw its relic-flower away
  Nor bid its music`s loitering echo speed.

Thou let`st the stranger`s glove lie where it fell;
If old things remain old things all is well,
  For thou art grateful as becomes man best
And hadst thou only heard me play one tune,
Or viewed me from a window, not so soon
  With thee would such things fade as with the rest.

I seem to see! We meet and part; `tis brief;
The book I opened keeps a folded leaf,
  The very chair I sat on, breaks the rank
That is a portrait of me on the wall—-
Three lines, my face comes at so slight a call:
  And for all this, one little hour to thank!

But now, because the hour through years was fixed,
Because our inmost beings met and mixed,
  Because thou once hast loved me—-wilt thou dare
Say to thy soul and Who may list beside,
``Therefore she is immortally my bride;
  ``Chance cannot change my love, nor time impair.

``So, what if in the dusk of life that`s left,
``I, a tired traveller of my sun bereft,
  Look from my path when, mimicking the same,
``The fire-fly glimpses past me, come and gone?
``—-Where was it till the sunset? where anon
  ``It will be at the sunrise! What`s to blame?``

Is it so helpful to thee? Canst thou take
The mimic up, nor, for the true thing`s sake,
  Put gently by such efforts at a beam?

Is the remainder of the way so long,
Thou need`st the little solace, thou the strong
  Watch out thy watch, let weak ones doze and dream!

—-Ah, but the fresher faces! ``Is it true,``
Thou`lt ask, ``some eyes are beautiful and new?
  ``Some hair,—-how can one choose but grasp such wealth?
``And if a man would press his lips to lips
``Fresh as the wilding hedge-rose-cup there slips
  ``The dew-drop out of, must it be by stealth?

``It cannot change the love still kept for Her,
``More than if such a picture I prefer
  ``Passing a day with, to a room`s bare side:
The painted form takes nothing she possessed,
Yet, while the Titian`s Venus lies at rest,
  A man looks. Once more, what is there to chide?``

So must I see, from where I sit and watch,
My own self sell myself, my hand attach
  Its warrant to the very thefts from me—-
Thy singleness of soul that made me proud,
Thy purity of heart I loved aloud,
  Thy man`s-truth I was bold to bid God see!

Love so, then, if thou wilt! Give all thou canst
Away to the new faces—-disentranced,
  (Say it and think it) obdurate no more:
Re-issue looks and words from the old mint,
Pass them afresh, no matter whose the print
  Image and superscription once they bore

Re-coin thyself and give it them to spend,—-
It all comes to the same thing at the end,
  Since mine thou wast, mine art and mine shalt be,
Faithful or faithless, scaling up the sum
Or lavish of my treasure, thou must come
  Back to the heart`s place here I keep for thee!

Only, why should it be with stain at all?
Why must I, 'twixt the leaves of coronal,
  Put any kiss of pardon on thy brow?
Why need the other women know so much,
And talk together, ``Such the look and such
  ``The smile he used to love with, then as now!``

Might I die last and show thee! Should I find
Such hardship in the few years left behind,
  If free to take and light my lamp, and go
Into thy tomb, and shut the door and sit,
Seeing thy face on those four sides of it
  The better that they are so blank, I know!

Why, time was what I wanted, to turn o'er
Within my mind each look, get more and more
  By heart each word, too much to learn at first;
And join thee all the fitter for the pause
'Neath the low doorway's lintel. That were cause
  For lingering, though thou calledst, if I durst!

And yet thou art the nobler of us two
What dare I dream of, that thou canst not do,
  Outstripping my ten small steps with one stride?
I'll say then, here's a trial and a task—-
Is it to bear?—-if easy, I'll not ask:
  Though love fail, I can trust on in thy pride.

Pride?—-when those eyes forestall the life behind
The death I have to go through!—-when I find,
  Now that I want thy help most, all of thee!
What did I fear? Thy love shall hold me fast
Until the little minute's sleep is past
  And I wake saved.—-And yet it will not be!

TWO IN THE CAMPAGNA

I wonder do you feel to-day
  As I have felt since, hand in hand,
We sat down on the grass, to stray
  In spirit better through the land,
This morn of Rome and May?

For me, I touched a thought, I know,
  Has tantalized me many times,
(Like turns of thread the spiders throw
  Mocking across our path) for rhymes
To catch at and let go.

Help me to hold it! First it left
  The yellowing fennel,<*1> run to seed
There, branching from the brickwork`s cleft,
  Some old tomb`s ruin: yonder weed
Took up the floating wet,

Where one small orange cup amassed
  Five beetles,—-blind and green they grope
Among the honey-meal: and last,
  Everywhere on the grassy slope
I traced it. Hold it fast!

The champaign with its endless fleece
  Of feathery grasses everywhere!
Silence and passion, joy and peace,
  An everlasting wash of air—-
Rome`s ghost since her decease.

Such life here, through such lengths of hours,
  Such miracles performed in play,
Such primal naked forms of flowers,

Such letting nature have her way
While heaven looks from its towers!

How say you? Let us, O my dove,
  Let us be unashamed of soul,
As earth lies bare to heaven above!
  How is it under our control
To love or not to love?

I would that you were all to me,
  You that are just so much, no more.
Nor yours nor mine, nor slave nor free!
  Where does the fault lie? What the core
O` the wound, since wound must be?

I would I could adopt your will,
  See with your eyes, and set my heart
Beating by yours, and drink my fill
  At your soul`s springs,—-your part my part
In life, for good and ill.

No. I yearn upward, touch you close,
  Then stand away. I kiss your cheek,
Catch your soul`s warmth,—-I pluck the rose
  And love it more than tongue can speak—-
Then the good minute goes.

Already how am I so far
  Out of that minute? Must I go
Still like the thistle-ball, no bar,
  Onward, whenever light winds blow,
Fixed by no friendly star?

Just when I seemed about to learn!
  Where is the thread now? Off again!
The old trick! Only I discern—-
  Infinite passion, and the pain
Of finite hearts that yearn.

* 1 Herb with yellow flowers and seeds supposed
* to be medicinal.

MISCONCEPTIONS

This is a spray the Bird clung to,
    Making it blossom with pleasure,
  Ere the high tree-top she sprang to,
    Fit for her nest and her treasure.
    Oh, what a hope beyond measure
Was the poor spray's, which the flying feet hung to, —-
So to be singled out, built in, and sung to!

  This is a heart the Queen leant on,
    Thrilled in a minute erratic,
  Ere the true bosom she bent on,
    Meet for love's regal dalmatic.<*1>
    Oh, what a fancy ecstatic
Was the poor heart's, ere the wanderer went on—-
Love to be saved for it, proffered to, spent on!

* 1 A vestment used by ecclesiastics, and formerly
* by senators and persons of high rank.

Dramatic Lyrics

A SERENADE AT THE VILLA

That was I, you heard last night,
  When there rose no moon at all,
Nor, to pierce the strained and tight
  Tent of heaven, a planet small:
Life was dead and so was light.

Not a twinkle from the fly,
  Not a glimmer from the worm;
When the crickets stopped their cry,
  When the owls forbore a term,
You heard music; that was I.

Earth turned in her sleep with pain,
  Sultrily suspired for proof:
In at heaven and out again,
  Lightning!—-where it broke the roof,
Bloodlike, some few drops of rain.

What they could my words expressed,
  O my love, my all, my one!
Singing helped the verses best,
  And when singing's best was done,
To my lute I left the rest.

So wore night; the East was gray,
  White the broad-faced hemlock-flowers:
There would be another day;
  Ere its first of heavy hours
Found me, I had passed away.

What became of all the hopes,
  Words and song and lute as well?
Say, this struck you—-``When life gropes

``Feebly for the path where fell
``Light last on the evening slopes,

``One friend in that path shall be,
  ``To secure my step from wrong;
``One to count night day for me,
  ``Patient through the watches long,
``Serving most with none to see.``

Never say—-as something bodes—-
  ``So, the worst has yet a worse!
``When life halts 'neath double loads,
  ``Better the taskmaster's curse
``Than such music on the roads!

``When no moon succeeds the sun,
  ``Nor can pierce the midnight's tent
``Any star, the smallest one,
  ``While some drops, where lightning rent,
``Show the final storm begun—-

``When the fire-fly hides its spot,
  ``When the garden-voices fail
``In the darkness thick and hot,—-
  ``Shall another voice avail,
``That shape be where these are not?

``Has some plague a longer lease,
  ``Proffering its help uncouth?
``Can't one even die in peace?
  ``As one shuts one's eyes on youth,
``Is that face the last one sees?``

Oh how dark your villa was,
  Windows fast and obdurate!
How the garden grudged me grass
  Where I stood—-the iron gate
Ground its teeth to let me pass!

ONE WAY OF LOVE

All June I bound the rose in sheaves.
Now, rose by rose, I strip the leaves
And strew them where Pauline may pass.
She will not turn aside? Alas!
Let them lie. Suppose they die?
The chance was they might take her eye.

How many a month I strove to suit
These stubborn fingers to the lute!
To-day I venture all I know.
She will not hear my music? So!
Break the string; fold music`s wing:
Suppose Pauline had bade me sing!

My whole life long I learned to love.
This hour my utmost art I prove
And speak my passion—-heaven or hell?
She will not give me heaven? `Tis well!
Lose who may—-I still can say,
Those who win heaven, blest are they!

ANOTHER WAY OF LOVE

June was not over
    Though past the fall,
  And the best of her roses
    Had yet to blow,
    When a man I know
  (But shall not discover,
    Since ears are dull,
  And time discloses)
Turned him and said with a man`s true air,
Half sighing a smile in a yawn, as `twere, —-
``If I tire of your June, will she greatly care?``

  Well, dear, in-doors with you!
    True! serene deadness
  Tries a man`s temper.
    What`s in the blossom
    June wears on her bosom?
  Can it clear scores with you?
    Sweetness and redness.
  Eadem semper!
Go, let me care for it greatly or slightly!
If June mend her bower now, your hand left unsightly
By plucking the roses, —-my June will do rightly.

  And after, for pastime,
    If June be refulgent
  With flowers in completeness,
    All petals, no prickles,
    Delicious as trickles
  Of wine poured at mass-time, —-
    And choose One indulgent
  To redness and sweetness:
Or if, with experience of man and of spider,

June use my June-lightning, the strong insect-ridder,
And stop the fresh film-work,—-why, June will consider.

A PRETTY WOMAN

That fawn-skin-dappled hair of hers,
    And the blue eye
    Dear and dewy,
And that infantine fresh air of hers!

To think men cannot take you, Sweet,
    And enfold you,
    Ay, and hold you,
And so keep you what they make you, Sweet!

You like us for a glance, you know —-
    For a word`s sake
    Or a sword`s sake,
All`s the same, whate`er the chance, you know.

And in turn we make you ours, we say —-
    You and youth too,
    Eyes and mouth too,
All the face composed of flowers, we say.

All`s our own, to make the most of, Sweet —-
    Sing and say for,
    Watch and pray for,
Keep a secret or go boast of, Sweet!

But for loving, why, you would not, Sweet,
    Though we prayed you,
    Paid you, brayed you
in a mortar —-for you could not, Sweet!

So, we leave the sweet face fondly there:
    Be its beauty
    Its sole duty!
Let all hope of grace beyond, lie there!

And while the face lies quiet there,
    Who shall wonder
    That I ponder
A conclusion? I will try it there.

As,—-why must one, for the love foregone,
    Scout mere liking?
    Thunder-striking
Earth,—-the heaven, we looked above for, gone!

Why, with beauty, needs there money be,
    Love with liking?
    Crush the fly-king
In his gauze, because no honey-bee?

May not liking be so simple-sweet,
    If love grew there
    'Twould undo there
All that breaks the cheek to dimples sweet?

Is the creature too imperfect,
    Would you mend it
    And so end it?
Since not all addition perfects aye!

Or is it of its kind, perhaps,
    Just perfection—-
    Whence, rejection
Of a grace not to its mind, perhaps?

Shall we burn up, tread that face at once
    Into tinder,
    And so hinder
Sparks from kindling all the place at once?

Or else kiss away one's soul on her?
    Your love-fancies!

—-A sick man sees
Truer, when his hot eyes roll on her!

Thus the craftsman thinks to grace the rose,—-
    Plucks a mould-flower
    For his gold flower,
Uses fine things that efface the rose:

Rosy rubies make its cup more rose,
    Precious metals
    Ape the petals,—-
Last, some old king locks it up, morose!

Then how grace a rose? I know a way!
    Leave it, rather.
    Must you gather?
Smell, kiss, wear it—-at last, throw away!

RESPECTABILITY

Dear, had the world in its caprice
  Deigned to proclaim ``I know you both,
  ``Have recognized your plighted troth,
Am sponsor for you: live in peace!``—-
How many precious months and years
  Of youth had passed, that speed so fast,
  Before we found it out at last,
The world, and what it fears?

How much of priceless life were spent
  With men that every virtue decks,
  And women models of their sex,
Society`s true ornament,—-
Ere we dared wander, nights like this,
  Thro` wind and rain, and watch the Seine,
  And feel the Boulevart break again
To warmth and light and bliss?

I know! the world proscribes not love;
  Allows my finger to caress
  Your lips` contour and downiness,
Provided it supply a glove.
The world`s good word!—-the Institute!
  Guizot receives Montalembert!
  Eh? Down the court three lampions flare:
Put forward your best foot!

LOVE IN A LIFE

Room after room,
I hunt the house through
We inhabit together.
Heart, fear nothing, for, heart, thou shalt find her —-
Next time, herself! —-not the trouble behind her
Left in the curtain, the couch`s perfume!
As she brushed it, the cornice-wreath blossomed anew:
Yon looking-glass gleaned at the wave of her feather.

Yet the day wears,
And door succeeds door;
I try the fresh fortune —-
Range the wide house from the wing to the centre.
Still the same chance! She goes out as I enter.
Spend my whole day in the quest, —-who cares?
But `tis twilight, you see, —-with such suites to explore,
Such closets to search, such alcoves to importune!

LIFE IN A LOVE

Escape me?
Never—-
Beloved!
While I am I, and you are you,
   So long as the world contains us both,
   Me the loving and you the loth
While the one eludes, must the other pursue.
My life is a fault at last, I fear:
   It seems too much like a fate, indeed!
   Though I do my best I shall scarce succeed.
But what if I fail of my purpose here?
It is but to keep the nerves at strain,
   To dry one's eyes and laugh at a fall,
And, baffled, get up and begin again,—-
   So the chace takes up one's life ` that's all.
While, look but once from your farthest bound
   At me so deep in the dust and dark,
No sooner the old hope goes to ground
   Than a new one, straight to the self-same mark,
I shape me—-
Ever
Removed!

IN THREE DAYS

So, I shall see her in three days
And just one night, but nights are short,
Then two long hours, and that is morn.
See how I come, unchanged, unworn!
Feel, where my life broke off from thine,
How fresh the splinters keep and fine, —-
Only a touch and we combine!

Too long, this time of year, the days!
But nights, at least the nights are short.
As night shows where ger one moon is,
A hand`s-breadth of pure light and bliss,
So life`s night gives my lady birth
And my eyes hold her! What is worth
The rest of heaven, the rest of earth?

O loaded curls, release your store
Of warmth and scent, as once before
The tingling hair did, lights and darks
Outbreaking into fairy sparks,
When under curl and curl I pried
After the warmth and scent inside,
Thro` lights and darks how manifold —-
The dark inspired, the light controlled
As early Art embrowns the gold.

What great fear, should one say, ``Three days
``That change the world might change as well
``Your fortune; and if joy delays,
``Be happy that no worse befell!``
What small fear, if another says,
``Three days and one short night beside
``May throw no shadow on your ways;
``But years must teem with change untried,

``With chance not easily defied,
``With an end somewhere undescried.``
No fear!—-or if a fear be born
This minute, it dies out in scorn.
Fear? I shall see her in three days
And one night, now the nights are short,
Then just two hours, and that is morn.

IN A YEAR

Never any more,
  While I live,
Need I hope to see his face
  As before.
Once his love grown chill,
  Mine may strive:
Bitterly we re-embrace,
  Single still.

Was it something said,
  Something done,
Vexed him? was it touch of hand,
  Turn of head?
Strange! that very way
  Love begun:
I as little understand
  Love's decay.

When I sewed or drew,
  I recall
How he looked as if I sung,
  —-Sweetly too.
If I spoke a word,
  First of all
Up his cheek the colour sprang,
  Then he heard.

Sitting by my side,
  At my feet,
So he breathed but air I breathed,
  Satisfied!
I, too, at love's brim
  Touched the sweet:

I would die if death bequeathed
  Sweet to him.

``Speak, I love thee best!``
  He exclaimed:
``Let thy love my own foretell!``
  I confessed:
``Clasp my heart on thine
  ``Now unblamed,
``Since upon thy soul as well
  ``Hangeth mine!``

Was it wrong to own,
  Being truth?
Why should all the giving prove
  His alone?
I had wealth and ease,
  Beauty, youth:
Since my lover gave me love,
  I gave these.

That was all I meant,
  —-To be just,
And the passion I had raised,
  To content.
Since he chose to change
  Gold for dust,
If I gave him what he praised
  Was it strange?

Would he loved me yet,
  On and on,
While I found some way undreamed
  —-Paid my debt!
Gave more life and more,
  Till, all gone,
He should smile ``She never seemed
  ``Mine before.

``What, she felt the while,
  ``Must I think?
``Love`s so different with us men!``
He should smile:
  ``Dying for my sake—-
``White and pink!
  ``Can`t we touch these bubbles then
``But they break?``

Dear, the pang is brief,
  Do thy part,
Have thy pleasure! How perplexed
  Grows belief!
Well, this cold clay clod
  Was man`s heart:
Crumble it, and what comes next?
  Is it God?

WOMEN AND ROSES

I dream of a red-rose tree.
And which of its roses three
Is the dearest rose to me?

Round and round, like a dance of snow
In a dazzling drift, as its guardians, go
Floating the women faded for ages,
Sculptured in stone, on the poet's pages.
Then follow women fresh and gay,
Living and loving and loved to-day.
Last, in the rear, flee the multitude of maidens,
Beauties yet unborn. And all, to one cadence,
They circle their rose on my rose tree.

Dear rose, thy term is reached,
Thy leaf hangs loose and bleached:
Bees pass it unimpeached.

Stay then, stoop, since I cannot climb,
You, great shapes of the antique time!
How shall I fix you, fire you, freeze you,
Break my heart at your feet to please you?
Oh, to possess and be possessed!
Hearts that beat 'neath each pallid breast!
Once but of love, the poesy, the passion,
Drink but once and die!—-In vain, the same fashion,
They circle their rose on my rose tree.

Dear rose, thy joy's undimmed,
Thy cup is ruby-rimmed,
Thy cup's heart nectar-brimmed.

Deep, as drops from a statue's plinth
The bee sucked in by the hyacinth,

So will I bury me while burning,
Quench like him at a plunge my yearning,
Eyes in your eyes, lips on your lips!
Fold me fast where the cincture slips,
Prison all my soul in eternities of pleasure,
Girdle me for once! But no—-the old measure,
They circle their rose on my rose tree.

Dear rose without a thorn,
Thy bud's the babe unborn:
First streak of a new morn.

Wings, lend wings for the cold, the clear!
What is far conquers what is near.
Roses will bloom nor want beholders,
Sprung from the dust where our flesh moulders.
What shall arrive with the cycle's change?
A novel grace and a beauty strange.
I will make an Eve, be the artist that began her,
Shaped her to his mind!—-Alas! in like manner
They circle their rose on my rose tree.

Dramatic Lyrics

BEFORE

Let them fight it out, friend! things have gone too far.
God must judge the couple: leave them as they are
—-Whichever one`s the guiltless, to his glory,
And whichever one the guilt`s with, to my story!

Why, you would not bid men, sunk in such a slough,
Strike no arm out further, stick and stink as now,
Leaving right and wrong to settle the embroilment,
Heaven with snaky hell, in torture and entoilment?

Who`s the culprit of them? How must he conceive
God—-the queen he caps to, laughing in his sleeve,
`` `Tis but decent to profess oneself beneath her:
``Still, one must not be too much in earnest, either!``

Better sin the whole sin, sure that God observes;
Then go live his life out! Life will try his nerves,
When the sky, which noticed all, makes no disclosure,
And the earth keeps up her terrible composure.

Let him pace at pleasure, past the walls of rose,
Pluck their fruits when grape-trees graze him as he goes!
For he `gins to guess the purpose of the garden,
With the sly mute thing, beside there, for a warden.

What`s the leopard-dog-thing, constant at his side,
A leer and lie in every eye of its obsequious hide?
When will come an end to all the mock obeisance,
And the price appear that pays for the misfeasance?

So much for the culprit. Who`s the martyred man?
Let him bear one stroke more, for be sure he can!
He that strove thus evil`s lump with good to leaven,
Let him give his blood at last and get his heaven!

All or nothing, stake it! Trust she God or no?
Thus far and no farther? farther? be it so!
Now, enough of your chicane of prudent pauses,
Sage provisos, sub-intents and saving-clauses!

Ah, ``forgive`` you bid him? While God`s champion lives,
Wrong shall be resisted: dead, why, he forgives.
But you must not end my friend ere you begin him;
Evil stands not crowned on earth, while breath is in him.

Once more—-Will the wronger, at this last of all,
Dare to say, ``I did wrong,`` rising in his fall?
No?—-Let go then! Both the fighters to their places!
While I count three, step you back as many paces!

AFTER

Take the cloak from his face, and at first
  Let the corpse do its worst!

How he lies in his rights of a man!
  Death has done all death can.
And, absorbed in the new life he leads,
  He recks not, he heeds
Nor his wrong nor my vengeance; both strike
  On his senses alike,
And are lost in the solemn and strange
  Surprise of the change.
Ha, what avails death to erase
  His offence, my disgrace?
I would we were boys as of old
  In the field, by the fold:
His outrage, God`s patience, man`s scorn
  Were so easily borne!

I stand here now, he lies in his place:
  Cover the face!

THE GUARDIAN-ANGEL

A PICTURE AT FANO

Dear and great Angel, wouldst thou only leave
  That child, when thou hast done with him, for me!
Let me sit all the day here, that when eve
  Shall find performed thy special ministry,
And time come for departure, thou, suspending
Thy flight, mayst see another child for tending,
  Another still, to quiet and retrieve.

Then I shall feel thee step one step, no more,
  From where thou standest now, to where I gaze,
—-And suddenly my head is covered o'er
  With those wings, white above the child who prays
Now on that tomb—-and I shall feel thee guarding
Me, out of all the world; for me, discarding
  Yon heaven thy home, that waits and opes its door.

I would not look up thither past thy head
  Because the door opes, like that child, I know,
For I should have thy gracious face instead,
  Thou bird of God! And wilt thou bend me low
Like him, and lay, like his, my hands together,
And lift them up to pray, and gently tether
  Me, as thy lamb there, with thy garment's spread?

If this was ever granted, I would rest
  My bead beneath thine, while thy healing hands
Close-covered both my eyes beside thy breast,
  Pressing the brain, which too much thought expands,
Back to its proper size again, and smoothing
Distortion down till every nerve had soothing,
  And all lay quiet, happy and suppressed.

How soon all worldly wrong would be repaired!
  I think how I should view the earth and skies
And sea, when once again my brow was bared
  After thy healing, with such different eyes.
O world, as God has made it! All is beauty:
And knowing this, is love, and love is duty.
  What further may be sought for or declared?

Guercino drew this angel I saw teach
  (Alfred, dear friend!)—-that little child to pray,
Holding the little hands up, each to each
  Pressed gently,—-with his own head turned away
Over the earth where so much lay before him
Of work to do, though heaven was opening o`er him,
  And he was left at Fano by the beach.

We were at Fano, and three times we went
  To sit and see him in his chapel there,
And drink his beauty to our soul`s content
  —-My angel with me too: and since I care
For dear Guercino`s fame (to which in power
And glory comes this picture for a dower,
  Fraught with a pathos so magnificent)—-

And since he did not work thus earnestly
  At all times, and has else endured some wrong—-
I took one thought his picture struck from me,
  And spread it out, translating it to song.
My love is here. Where are you, dear old friend?
How rolls the Wairoa at your world`s far end?
  This is Ancona, yonder is the sea.

MEMORABILIA

Ah, did you once see Shelley plain,
  And did he stop and speak to you
And did you speak to him again?
  How strange it seems and new!

But you were living before that,
  And also you are living after;
And the memory I started at—-
  My starting moves your laughter.

I crossed a moor, with a name of its own
  And a certain use in the world no doubt,
Yet a hand`s-breadth of it shines alone
  `Mid the blank miles round about:

For there I picked up on the heather
  And there I put inside my breast
A moulted feather, an eagle-feather!
  Well, I forget the rest.

POPULARITY

Stand still, true poet that you are!
  I know you; let me try and draw you.
Some night you`ll fail us: when afar
  You rise, remember one man saw you,
Knew you, and named a star!

My star, God`s glow-worm! Why extend
  That loving hand of his which leads you
Yet locks you safe from end to end
  Of this dark world, unless he needs you,
just saves your light to spend?

His clenched hand shall unclose at last,
  I know, and let out all the beauty:
My poet holds the future fast,
  Accepts the coming ages` duty,
Their present for this past.

That day, the earth`s feast-master`s brow
  Shall clear, to God the chalice raising;
``Others give best at first, but thou
  ``Forever set`st our table praising,
``Keep`st the good wine till now!``

Meantime, I`ll draw you as you stand,
  With few or none to watch and wonder:
I`ll say —-a fisher, on the sand
  By Tyre the old, with ocean-plunder,
A netful, brought to land.

Who has not heard how Tyrian shells
  Enclosed the blue, that dye of dyes
Whereof one drop worked miracles,

113

And coloured like Astarte`s<*1> eyes
Raw silk the merchant sells?

And each bystander of them all
  Could criticize, and quote tradition
How depths of blue sublimed some pall
  —-To get which, pricked a king`s ambition
Worth sceptre, crown and ball.

Yet there`s the dye, in that rough mesh,
  The sea has only just o`erwhispered!
Live whelks, each lip`s beard dripping fresh,
  As if they still the water`s lisp heard
Through foam the rock-weeds thresh.

Enough to furnish Solomon
  Such hangings for his cedar-house,
That, when gold-robed he took the throne
  In that abyss of blue, the Spouse
Might swear his presence shone

Most like the centre-spike of gold
  Which burns deep in the blue-bell`s womb,
What time, with ardours manifold,
  The bee goes singing to her groom,
Drunken and overbold.

Mere conchs! not fit for warp or woof!
  Till cunning come to pound and squeeze
And clarify,—-refine to proof
  The liquor filtered by degrees,
While the world stands aloof.

And there`s the extract, flasked and fine,
  And priced and saleable at last!
And Hobbs, Nobbs, Stokes and Nokes combine
  To paint the future from the past,
Put blue into their line.

Hobbs hints blue,—-Straight he turtle eats:
  Nobbs prints blue,—-claret crowns his cup:
Nokes outdares Stokes in azure feats,—-
  Both gorge. Who fished the murex<*2> up?
What porridge had John Keats?

* 1 The Syrian Venus.
* 2 Molluscs from which the famous Tyrian
* purple dye was obtained

MASTER HUGUES OF SAXE-GOTHA

Hist, but a word, fair and soft!
  Forth and be judged, Master Hugues!
Answer the question I`ve put you so oft:
  What do you mean by your mountainous fugues?<*1>
See, we`re alone in the loft, —-

I, the poor organist here,
  Hugues, the composer of note,
Dead though, and done with, this many a year:
  Let`s have a colloquy, something to quote,
Make the world prick up its ear!

See, the church empties apace:
  Fast they extinguish the lights.
Hallo there, sacristan! Five minutes` grace!
  Here`s a crank pedal wants setting to rights,
Baulks one of holding the base.

See, our huge house of the sounds,
  Hushing its hundreds at once,
Bids the last loiterer back to his bounds!
  O you may challenge them, not a response
Get the church-saints on their rounds!

(Saints go their rounds, who shall doubt?
  —-March, with the moon to admire,
Up nave, down chancel, turn transept about,
  Supervise all betwixt pavement and spire,
Put rats and mice to the rout—-

Aloys and Jurien and Just—-
  Order things back to their place,
Have a sharp eye lest the candlesticks rust,

116

Rub the church-plate, darn the sacrament-lace,
Clear the desk-velvet of dust.)

Here`s your book, younger folks shelve!
  Played I not off-hand and runningly,
Just now, your masterpiece, hard number twelve?
  Here`s what should strike, could one handle it cunningly:
Help the axe, give it a helve!

Page after page as I played,
  Every bar`s rest, where one wipes
Sweat from one`s brow, I looked up and surveyed,
  O`er my three claviers<*2> yon forest of pipes
Whence you still peeped in the shade.

Sure you were wishful to speak?
  You, with brow ruled like a score,
Yes, and eyes buried in pits on each cheek,
  Like two great breves,<*3> as they wrote them of yore,
Each side that bar, your straight beak!

Sure you said—-``Good, the mere notes!
  ``Still, couldst thou take my intent,
``Know what procured me our Company`s votes—-
  ``A master were lauded and sciolists shent,
``Parted the sheep from the goats!``

Well then, speak up, never flinch!
  Quick, ere my candle`s a snuff
—-Burnt, do you see? to its uttermost inch—-
  I believe in you, but that`s not enough:
Give my conviction a clinch!

First you deliver your phrase
  —-Nothing propound, that I see,
Fit in itself for much blame or much praise—-
  Answered no less, where no answer needs be:
Off start the Two on their ways.

Straight must a Third interpose,
  Volunteer needlessly help;
In strikes a Fourth, a Fifth thrusts in his nose,
  So the cry`s open, the kennel`s a-yelp,
Argument`s hot to the close.

One dissertates, he is candid;
  Two must discept, —has distinguished;
Three helps the couple, if ever yet man did;
  Four protests; Five makes a dart at the thing wished:
Back to One, goes the case bandied.

One says his say with a difference
  More of expounding, explaining!
All now is wrangle, abuse, and vociferance;
  Now there`s a truce, all`s subdued, self-restraining:
Five, though, stands out all the stiffer hence.

One is incisive, corrosive:
  Two retorts, nettled, curt, crepitant;
Three makes rejoinder, expansive, explosive;
  Four overbears them all, strident and strepitant,
Five ... O Danaides,<*4> O Sieve!

Now, they ply axes and crowbars;
  Now, they prick pins at a tissue
Fine as a skein of the casuist Escobar`s<*5>
  Worked on the bone of a lie. To what issue?
Where is our gain at the Two-bars?

Est fuga, volvitur rota.
  On we drift: where looms the dim port?
One, Two, Three, Four, Five, contribute their quota;
  Something is gained, if one caught but the import—-
Show it us, Hugues of Saxe-Gotha!

What with affirming, denying,
  Holding, risposting,<*6> subjoining,

All`s like ... it`s like ... for an instance I`m trying ...
　There! See our roof, its gilt moulding and groining
Under those spider-webs lying!

So your fugue broadens and thickens,
Greatens and deepens and lengthens,
Till we exclaim—-``But where`s music, the dickens?
``Blot ye the gold, while your spider-web strengthens
``—-Blacked to the stoutest of tickens?``<*7>

I for man`s effort am zealous:
　Prove me such censure unfounded!
Seems it surprising a lover grows jealous—-
　Hopes `twas for something, his organ-pipes sounded,
Tiring three boys at the bellows?

Is it your moral of Life?
　Such a web, simple and subtle,
Weave we on earth here in impotent strife,
　Backward and forward each throwing his shuttle,
Death ending all with a knife?

Over our heads truth and nature—-
　Still our life`s zigzags and dodges,
Ins and outs, weaving a new legislature—-
　God`s gold just shining its last where that lodges,
Palled beneath man`s usurpature.

So we o`ershroud stars and roses,
Cherub and trophy and garland;
Nothings grow something which quietly closes
Heaven`s earnest eye: not a glimpse of the far land
Gets through our comments and glozes.

Ah but traditions, inventions,
　(Say we and make up a visage)
So many men with such various intentions,

Down the past ages, must know more than this age!
Leave we the web its dimensions!

Who thinks Hugues wrote for the deaf,
  Proved a mere mountain in labour?
Better submit; try again; what`s the clef?
  `Faith, `tis no trifle for pipe and for tabor—-
Four flats, the minor in F.

Friend, your fugue taxes the finger
  Learning it once, who would lose it?
Yet all the while a misgiving will linger,
  Truth`s golden o`er us although we refuse it—-
Nature, thro` cobwebs we string her.

Hugues! I advise *Me Pn*
  (Counterpoint glares like a Gorgon)
Bid One, Two, Three, Four, Five, clear the arena!
  Say the word, straight I unstop the full-organ,
Blare out the *mode Palestrina.*<*8>

While in the roof, if I`m right there,
  ... Lo you, the wick in the socket!
Hallo, you sacristan, show us a light there!
  Down it dips, gone like a rocket.
What, you want, do you, to come unawares,
Sweeping the church up for first morning-prayers,
And find a poor devil has ended his cares
At the foot of your rotten-runged rat-riddled stairs?
  Do I carry the moon in my pocket?

* 1 A fugue is a short melody.
* 2 Keyboard of organ.
* 3 A note in music.
* 4 The daughters of Danaus, condemned to pour water
* into a sieve.
* 5 The Spanish casuist, so severely mauled by Pascal.
* 6 A quick return in fencing.

* 7 A closely woven fabric.
* 8 *Giovanni P. da Palestrina,* celebrated musician (1524-1594).